WILD
OCEANS

WILD
OCEANS

Camilla de la Bedoyere

Steve Parker

Miles
KeLLy

First published in 2011 by Miles Kelly Publishing Ltd
Harding's Barn, Bardfield End Green, Thaxted, Essex, CM6 3PX, UK

Copyright © Miles Kelly Publishing Ltd 2011

2 4 6 8 10 9 7 5 3 1

Publishing Director Belinda Gallagher
Creative Director Jo Cowan
Editorial Director Rosie McGuire
Editors Carly Blake, Sarah Parkin, Claire Philip
Cover Designer Simon Lee
Designers Joe Jones, Andrea Slane
Additional Design Kayleigh Allen
Image Manager Liberty Newton
Indexers Gill Lee, Jane Parker
Production Manager Elizabeth Collins
Reprographics Stephan Davis, Jennifer Hunt, Ian Paulyn

ISBN 978-1-84810-465-5

Printed in China

British Library Cataloguing-in-Publication Data
A catalogue record for this book is available from the British Library

Made with paper from a sustainable forest

www.mileskelly.net   info@mileskelly.net

www.factsforprojects.com

Self-publish your
children's book

buddingpress.co.uk

CONTENTS

DEEP OCEAN

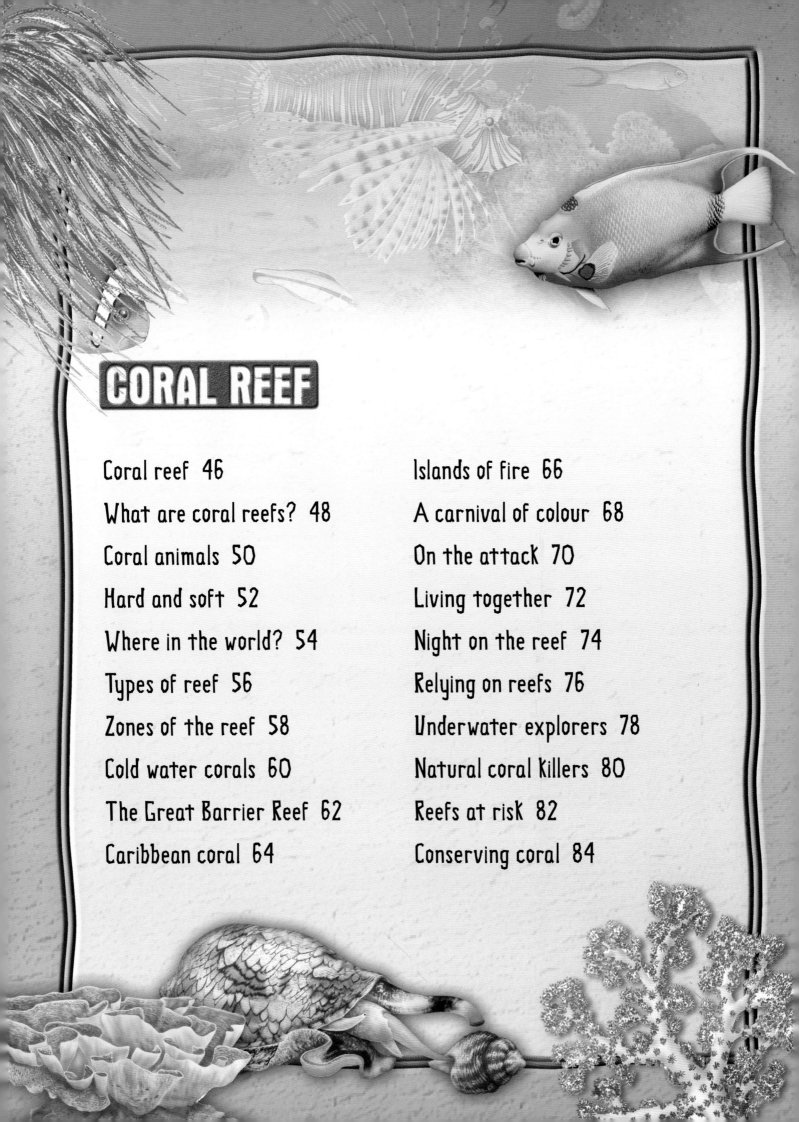

CORAL REEF

SEASHORE

DEEP OCEAN

Far down in the dark waters of the deep oceans lies a mysterious wilderness. The deep ocean is a place without light, where the water pressure can crush human bones. Until modern times, people did not believe that anything could live here. Now scientists are discovering new creatures all the time, from colossal squid with huge eyes to giant worms that are 2 metres in length.

▶ Almost 2.5 kilometres below the surface of the ocean, an eelpout fish hides among giant tube worms and crabs at a hydrothermal vent. Only two people have been to the deepest part of the oceans, which is about 11 kilometres below the waves. In contrast, 12 human explorers have walked on the surface of the Moon, which is 384,400 kilometres from Earth.

The ocean zones

Oceans are enormous areas of water. They cover more than two-thirds of the Earth's surface. There are five oceans and they make up a giant ecosystem of creatures that depend on seawater to survive.

ARCTIC OCEAN

PACIFIC OCEAN

ARCTIC OCEAN

ATLANTIC OCEAN

PACIFIC OCEAN

PACIFIC OCEAN

INDIAN OCEAN

SOUTHERN OCEAN

ATLANTIC OCEAN

SOUTHERN OCEAN

Jellyfish

LIGHT ZONE 0- 200 metres

TWILIGHT ZONE 200-1000 metres

DARK ZONE 1000-4000 metres

Sea lily

ABYSSAL ZONE 4000-6000 metres

Tube worms

HADAL ZONE 6000-10,000 metres

At their edges, oceans are shallow and teem with life. These places are called continental shelves. However continental shelves only take up 5 percent of the total area of the oceans. The shelves fall away into deep slopes and from there, the seabed stretches out as dark, enormous plains.

◄▲ There are five oceans. They are all connected and make up one giant mass of water.

▶ Scientists divide the ocean into five layers, or zones. Different types of animals live in the different zones.

DELIGHT IN LIGHT
Find out about the wavelengths of white light. How many colours make up white light, and what are they? Find the answers by searching on the Internet with the keywords 'rainbow' and 'light'.

Coral

Bluefin tuna

Plankton

Octopus

Wolf eel

Hatchet fish

Squid

Gulper eel

Fangtooth

Viperfish

Rattail

Hagfish

Deep-sea angler

Amphipods

Sea cucumber

Oceans are deep places. The average depth is 3800 metres, but in some places the seabed lies as deep as 11,000 metres. If all the water in the oceans was removed, a dramatic landscape would be revealed – giant mountains, volcanoes, smooth flat plains and deep trenches.

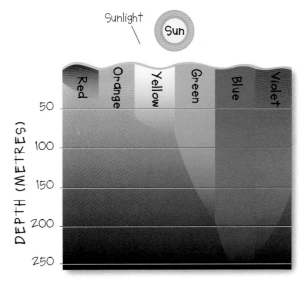

Sunlight

Sun

Red | Orange | Yellow | Green | Blue | Violet

DEPTH (METRES)

50

100

150

200

250

▲ Sunlight can only pass through the ocean's uppermost layer. Everything below is in perpetual darkness.

Sunlight streams through the upper zone of the ocean, giving warmth, light and energy to the creatures that live there. This is called the Light Zone. Light is made up of many colours, and as it passes through water, the colours get absorbed, until only blue light is left. At a depth of around 200 metres, all blue light has disappeared and in the zones below, darkness takes over.

In deep water

Living in water is nothing like living in air. The ocean is one of Earth's most remarkable habitats. Ocean water is constantly moving and changing. The creatures that live here have to cope without light, and the weight of many tonnes of water above them.

As you travel deeper into the ocean you will feel a great weight on your body. Water is 830 times denser than air, and it is very heavy. It is water's density that helps things to float, or stay buoyant. However, the further down you go, the more pressure the water forces on you.

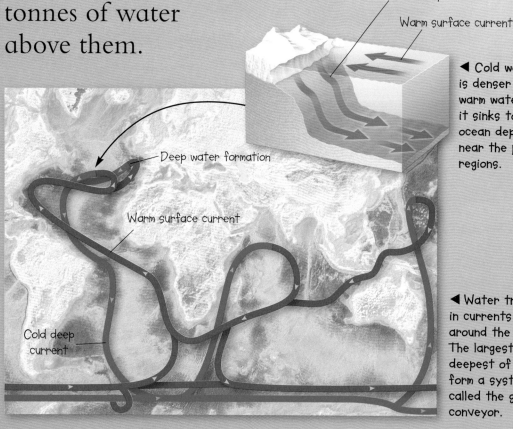

Cold deep current

Warm surface current

Deep water formation

Warm surface current

Cold deep current

◄ Cold water is denser than warm water, and it sinks to the ocean depths near the polar regions.

◄ Water travels in currents around the world. The largest and deepest of these form a system called the global conveyor.

DEPTH (METRES)

0 — 1 atm

10 — 2 atm

20 — 3 atm

30 — 4 atm

40 — 5 atm

► Water pressure is measured in atmospheres (atm). Pressure increases with depth, squashing the molecules of air in this balloon.

At the surface, wind creates waves and the Moon's gravitational pull causes tides. Further down, other forces are in action. Ocean water is continually moving, passing around the globe in giant streams called currents. If you were to get caught in one of these strong, deep currents, after 1000 years you would have journeyed all around the world!

Although you will soon be cold, you may notice that the temperature of the water around you doesn't change much. Ocean water has great heat capacity, which means that it warms up slowly and cools down slowly too. It can hold on to its temperature about 4000 times better than air can.

▼ Many enormous animals, such as this basking shark, live in the ocean. The dense, salty seawater supports their great weight.

The good news is that you won't have to work hard to get food. If you stay still, it will float right past your nose. Because water is dense, tiny creatures and particles of food are suspended in it. Some sea creatures can wave tentacles to catch food, or just open their mouths as they swim!

◀ A magnified view of plankton, tiny animals and plants that float or swim in seawater. They often become food for bigger animals.

MAKING WATER HEAVY

You will need:

two identical cups containing the same amount of water   salt

Add salt to one of the cups and stir. Continue until no more salt will dissolve. Weigh both cups – the salty one should be heavier. Salty water is denser and heavier than fresh water.

You should never drink seawater. It has lots of minerals, called salts, dissolved in it. A single bath of seawater contains 2.8 kilograms of salts. Most of that is sodium chloride (common salt). Gases, such as oxygen and nitrogen are also dissolved in seawater.

▶ A beaker of ocean water may look dirty, but it is full of substances that are food for tiny organisms called phytoplankton.

Other elements 0.6%
Sodium 1%
Chloride 1.9%
Water 96.5%
Salt 3.5%

The Light Zone

The top 200 metres of the ocean is called the Light Zone. At the continental shelf, sunlight can reach all the way to the seabed. However within 10 metres of the water's surface, nearly all of the red parts of light have been absorbed, which means that many creatures appear dull in colour.

▲ The shiny scales on tuna fish reflect sunlight as they dart from side to side, to confuse their predators.

▶ Green turtles have to visit the surface to breathe air, then they dive to feed on marine plants.

Sunlight provides the energy for plants to grow. Marine plants such as seaweed need light in order to make food from carbon dioxide and water, in a process called photosynthesis. Plants also produce oxygen, the gas we breathe, and without it there would be no life in the oceans.

◀ Marine plants, including seaweed (shown here) and phytoplankton, are called algae.

◄ Emperor penguins can stay underwater for up to 20 minutes at a time, hunting for fish.

Many marine plants are almost invisible. They are called phytoplankton and are so tiny that they have to be viewed with a microscope. Phytoplankton begin a food web that supports nearly all ocean life. They are eaten by microscopic animals, called zooplankton, and bigger animals too.

I DON'T BELIEVE IT!

Six billion tonnes of phytoplankton grow in the Light Zone every year and they produce half of the oxygen in our atmosphere. Without them there would be almost no animal life in the oceans, and few animals on land either.

The Light Zone is bright and full of food, making it a busy habitat. Fish such as anchovies and sardines come to feed on swarms of plankton. In turn larger animals, such as sharks, come to prey upon the fish. Even birds, such as pelicans and penguins, enter this habitat to grab what food they can.

Most swimming animals of the Light Zone can move into deeper water to escape from predators. At around a depth of 200 metres almost all sunlight has been absorbed and darkness takes over in the Twilight Zone.

▼ Warm-water corals need sunlight to grow, and they build reefs in the Light Zone.

The Twilight Zone

From a depth of 200 to 1000 metres lies the Twilight Zone. Just enough light reaches this zone for animals to see, and be seen by. Predators and prey battle it out in a constant fight for survival.

Siphuncle

Jaws

Digestive gland

Stomach

Brain

Gonad

Tentacles

Funnel

Gills

Heart

▲ A nautilus fills the chambers in its shell with water or gas by a tube called a siphuncle. Like octopuses and squid, a nautilus propels itself by pushing water out of its funnel.

Mighty sperm whales plunge into the Twilight Zone when they are hunting squid. They can dive to depths of 1000 metres and hold their breath for up to 90 minutes at a time. The deepest known dive of any sperm whale was 3000 metres, and the whale swam at a speed of 4 metres a second to get there!

The nautilus can swim, float and move up and down in the Twilight Zone. It lives in the outermost chamber of its shell, and its inner chambers are filled with gas or liquid. By pushing gas into the chambers, liquid is forced out and the nautilus becomes lighter – and floats up. When the gas is replaced with liquid, the nautilus sinks.

◄ Huge sperm whales are mammals, which means they have to return to the surface to breathe.

It is hard to see if your eyes are deep inside your head. Barreleye fish don't mind because they have see-through heads. They swim with their big, green eyes peering upwards. When the fish sees its prey, it flips its body upright and rotates its eyes in its head. This allows the fish to keep its prey in view while swimming up to grab it.

Eye

Mouth   Nostril

◄ A barreleye fish's eyes are very sensitive, which help it to spot its prey in low light.

▼ Comb jellies swim by beating rows of comb-like plates, which bend light rays to make colourful shimmers.

There are few hard surfaces to attach to, so animals in the Twilight Zone are mostly floaters and swimmers. Many have unusual shapes and their bodies are often soft and watery. Comb jellies are soft-bodied animals, but they can turn hard by contracting muscles. Some have long, sticky tentacles to grab prey.

▼ Sea pens anchor themselves to the seafloor in the Twilight Zone. They feed on plankton by catching it in their feathery branches.

TRUE OR FALSE?

1. Barreleye fish have see-through heads.
2. Sperm whales can breathe underwater.
3. Nautiluses swim using fins.
4. The Twilight Zone is pitch black.

Answers:
1. True 2. False 3. False 4. False

Monster of the deep

Giant squid are monsters of the deep. They can grow to 15 metres in length, including tentacles, which alone can grow to 12 metres. Their eyes are thought to be the largest of any animal. Each one is up to 40 centimetres in diameter!

Little is known about these mysterious animals because they live in the Twilight Zone. Giant squid can swim well, and with their good eyesight they can spot fishing nets and move swiftly away. Very few have ever been caught, and what is known about them has been revealed from dead specimens, or remains that have been found in the stomachs of sperm whales.

▶ Giant squid have a reputation as fearsome monsters. In fact, they are more likely to be gentle giants of the deep.

ANIMAL GIANTS

Put these animal giants in order of size, from largest to smallest:
African elephant
Hercules beetle
Blue whale   Giant squid

Answer:
Blue whale, giant squid,
African elephant, Hercules beetle

Teeth

Sucker

Tentacle

Eye

Beak

Arm

People have known about giant squid for hundreds of years. The first one to be recorded was found in Iceland in 1639, and the stories and myths began. People feared that these creatures could sink ships or grab people on deck. When sperm whales were discovered with scars caused by giant squid suckers, people realized that these predators battle with large whales.

Giant squid are predators. No one knows for sure how they live, but like other squid they probably hunt fish, octopuses and smaller squid. Their muscular tentacles are equipped with giant, toothed suckers that can grab hold of wriggly prey.

▶ The eye of a giant squid has a diameter bigger than a person's head.

The Dark Zone

Below 1000 metres absolutely no light can penetrate. So far from the Sun's rays, this habitat is intensely cold, and there is bone-crushing pressure from the enormous weight of water above. It is called the Dark Zone, and it extends to 4000 metres below the ocean's surface.

It snows in the Dark Zone! Billions of particles fall down towards the seabed, and this is called marine snow. This 'snow' is made up of droppings from animals above, and animals and plants that have died. Small flakes often collect together to become larger and heavier, drifting down up to 200 metres a day. Marine snow is an important source of food for billions of deep-sea creatures.

▲ Fierce-looking fangtooth fish can swim to depths of around 5000 metres, into the Abyssal Zone, when they follow their prey.

I DON'T BELIEVE IT!

The orange roughy lives in deep water where its colour appears black if any light reaches it. This is believed to be one of the longest living fish — one individual allegedly reached 149 years of age.

A fangtooth fish may have enormous teeth, but at only 15 centimetres in length, these fish are not as scary as they sound. Fangtooths have poor eyesight, and in the Dark Zone other senses are just as valuable. These fish can detect tiny movements in the surrounding water, which they follow to find their prey.

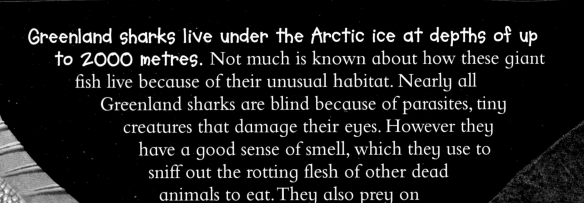

Greenland sharks live under the Arctic ice at depths of up to 2000 metres. Not much is known about how these giant fish live because of their unusual habitat. Nearly all Greenland sharks are blind because of parasites, tiny creatures that damage their eyes. However they have a good sense of smell, which they use to sniff out the rotting flesh of other dead animals to eat. They also prey on seals and other sharks.

▲ Greenland sharks can grow to 6 metres long. They live in the Arctic and often swim close to shore, but pose little threat to humans.

▼ Giant isopods are crustaceans that live in the Dark Zone. They are related to crabs, shrimps, lobsters and woodlice, and can reach a length of 35 centimetres. Isopods have long antennae that help them feel their way in the dark.

Giant isopods are peculiar crawling creatures that look like huge woodlice. Their bodies are protected by tough plates, and they can roll themselves up into a ball when they come under attack. Isopods live on the seabed, searching for soft-bodied animals to eat.

The Abyssal Zone

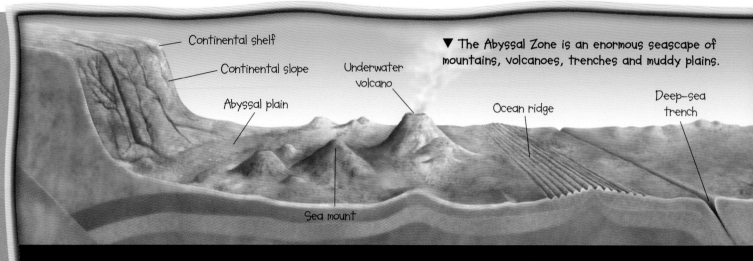

Continental shelf

Continental slope

Underwater volcano

Abyssal plain

▼ The Abyssal Zone is an enormous seascape of mountains, volcanoes, trenches and muddy plains.

Ocean ridge

Deep-sea trench

Sea mount

Below the Dark Zone is the Abyssal Zone, or abyss, which reaches from 4000 to 6000 metres. Where the continental slope ends, the sea floor stretches out in a giant plain. Around one-third of the seabed is in the Abyssal Zone.

The abyssal plains have mountains (called sea mounts), trenches and valleys. Many sea mounts are drowned volcanoes, and there may be 30,000 of them in the world's oceans. The sides of the mounts are sheer, which causes water to flow upwards in a process called upwelling. This flow of water brings nutrients to the area, and many animals live in these habitats.

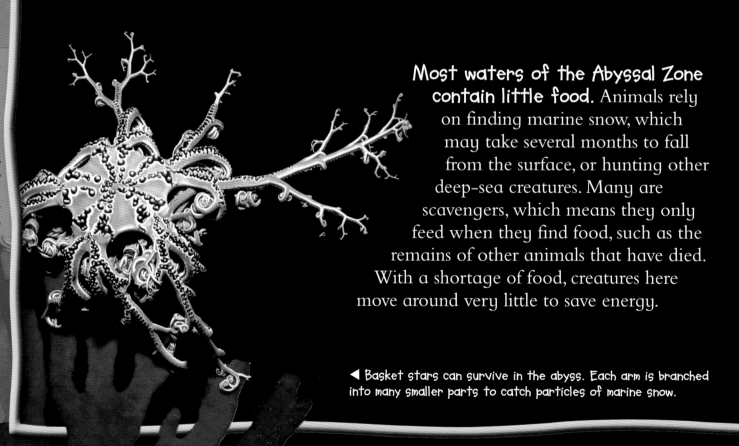

Most waters of the Abyssal Zone contain little food. Animals rely on finding marine snow, which may take several months to fall from the surface, or hunting other deep-sea creatures. Many are scavengers, which means they only feed when they find food, such as the remains of other animals that have died. With a shortage of food, creatures here move around very little to save energy.

◄ Basket stars can survive in the abyss. Each arm is branched into many smaller parts to catch particles of marine snow.

▼ There are around 60 types of hagfish. They have eel-like bodies with four hearts, but no bones.

An Atlantic hagfish is a slimy, fish-like animal of the abyss with disgusting eating habits. It is nearly blind but has a good sense of smell, which helps it to find prey. A hagfish has tentacles and hooks around its mouth to grab hold of its victim's flesh. Then it burrows into the prey's body, eating its insides. A hagfish can survive for many months without feeding again.

The most common fish in the Abyssal Zone are called rattails, or grenadiers. There are around 300 different types of rattails in the world and scientists estimate that there are at least 20 billion of just one type – that's more than three times the number of humans!

▼ Rattails are slow movers so they probably creep up on their prey to catch them. They are also scavengers, eating anything they can find on the seabed. Here, they swarm around a bait cage and the submersible *Mir I*.

23

Glass in the abyss

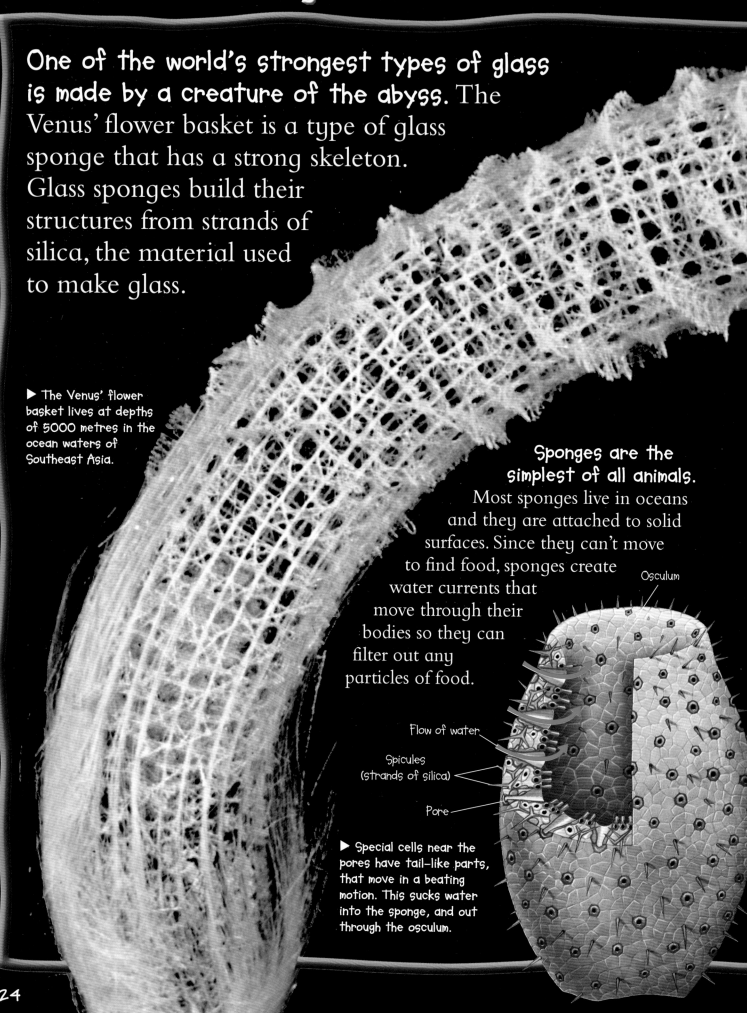

One of the world's strongest types of glass is made by a creature of the abyss. The Venus' flower basket is a type of glass sponge that has a strong skeleton. Glass sponges build their structures from strands of silica, the material used to make glass.

▶ The Venus' flower basket lives at depths of 5000 metres in the ocean waters of Southeast Asia.

Sponges are the simplest of all animals. Most sponges live in oceans and they are attached to solid surfaces. Since they can't move to find food, sponges create water currents that move through their bodies so they can filter out any particles of food.

Osculum

Flow of water

Spicules (strands of silica)

Pore

▶ Special cells near the pores have tail-like parts, that move in a beating motion. This sucks water into the sponge, and out through the osculum.

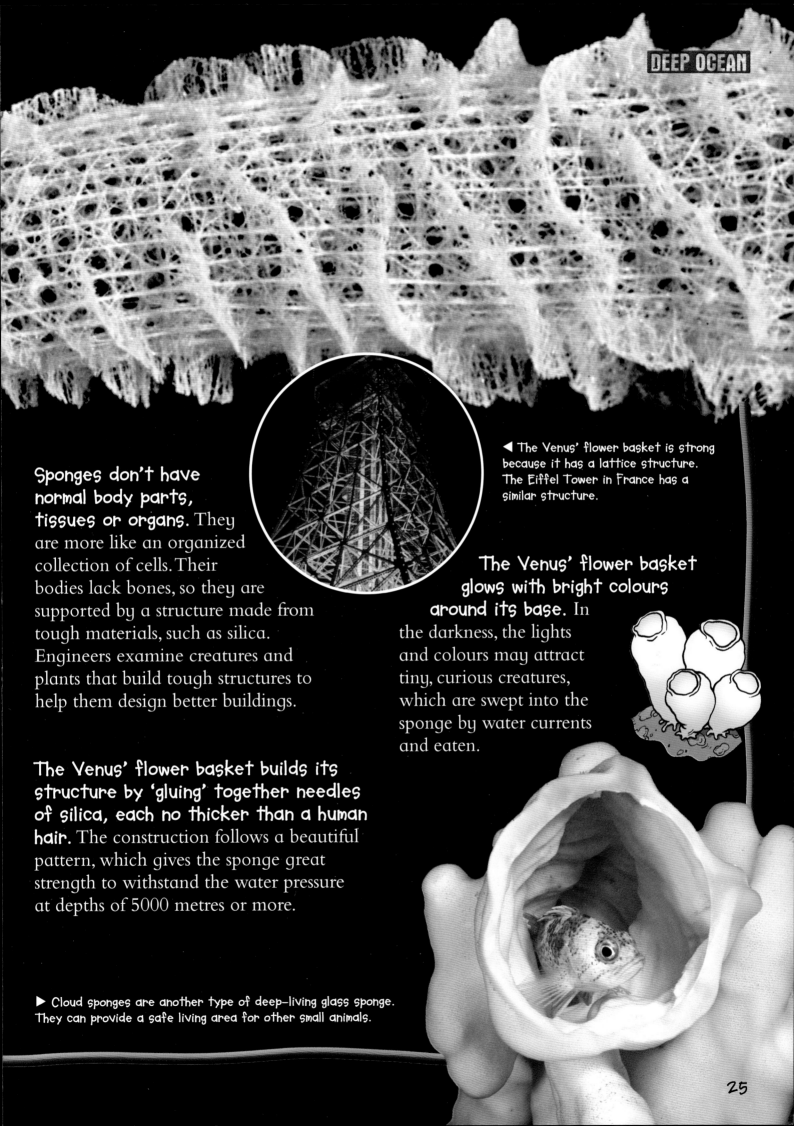

▲ The Venus' flower basket is strong because it has a lattice structure. The Eiffel Tower in France has a similar structure.

Sponges don't have normal body parts, tissues or organs. They are more like an organized collection of cells. Their bodies lack bones, so they are supported by a structure made from tough materials, such as silica. Engineers examine creatures and plants that build tough structures to help them design better buildings.

The Venus' flower basket glows with bright colours around its base. In the darkness, the lights and colours may attract tiny, curious creatures, which are swept into the sponge by water currents and eaten.

The Venus' flower basket builds its structure by 'gluing' together needles of silica, each no thicker than a human hair. The construction follows a beautiful pattern, which gives the sponge great strength to withstand the water pressure at depths of 5000 metres or more.

▶ Cloud sponges are another type of deep-living glass sponge. They can provide a safe living area for other small animals.

The Hadal Zone

The oceans plunge to depths greater than 6000 metres in only a few places, called trenches. This is called the Hadal Zone, named after the Greek word 'hades', which means 'unseen'. It's the perfect name for the most mysterious habitat on Earth.

Mariana Trench 11,034 metres

Tonga Trench 10,882 metres

Philippine Trench 10,540 metres

Kuril-Kamchatka Trench 10,500 metres

Kermadec Trench 10,047 metres

Bonin Trench 9994 metres

New Britain Trench 9940 metres

Izu Trench 9780 metres

Mount Everest 8850 metres

▲ Earth's largest mountain, Everest, could fit into eight of the world's deepest trenches.

The deepest of all trenches is the Mariana Trench in the Pacific Ocean, which plunges to 11,034 metres. It is 2550 kilometres long and about 70 kilometres wide. This trench was created when two massive plates in the Earth's crust collided millions of years ago.

Scientists know very little about animals that live in the Hadal Zone. Collecting live animals from this depth causes great problems because their bodies are suited to high water pressure. When they are brought to the surface the pressure drops, and they die.

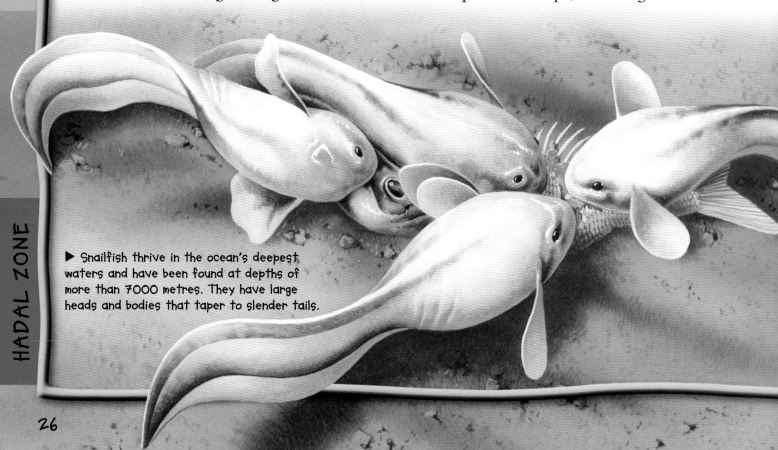

▶ Snailfish thrive in the ocean's deepest waters and have been found at depths of more than 7000 metres. They have large heads and bodies that taper to slender tails.

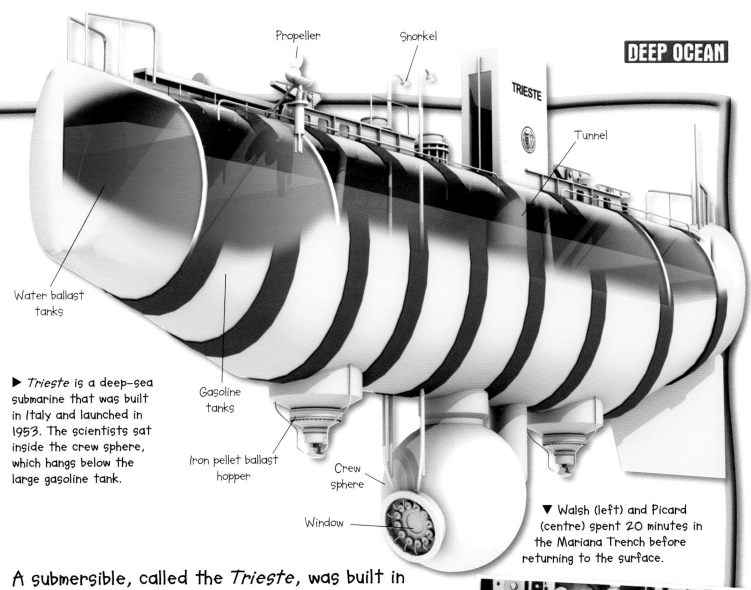

Propeller

Snorkel

TRIESTE

Tunnel

Water ballast tanks

Gasoline tanks

Iron pellet ballast hopper

Crew sphere

Window

▶ *Trieste* is a deep-sea submarine that was built in Italy and launched in 1953. The scientists sat inside the crew sphere, which hangs below the large gasoline tank.

▼ Walsh (left) and Picard (centre) spent 20 minutes in the Mariana Trench before returning to the surface.

A submersible, called the *Trieste*, was built in the 1950s, which could dive to the Hadal Zone.
In 1960, explorers Don Walsh and Jacques Piccard climbed aboard and began one of the most dangerous journeys ever undertaken. It took five hours to descend to 10,911 metres in the Mariana Trench and here they saw the deepest-known crustacean – a red shrimp. Other similar creatures called amphipods have been collected at depths of 10,500 metres.

CURIOUS CREATURES

Draw a picture of your own Hadal Zone creature. It should probably be dark-coloured, with tiny eyes, or none at all, and very ugly. Body parts that help it feel its way around a dark habitat would be helpful.

The deepest-living fish are believed to belong to a family called *Abyssobrotula*.
One fish, *Abyssobrotula galatheae*, was captured in 1970 at a depth of 8370 metres. It was found by explorers in the Puerto Rico Trench. Scientists tried to bring the fish to the surface, but it did not survive the journey.

Muds and oozes

The remains of all marine creatures eventually get eaten or drift down to the seabed. These remains, which are mostly marine snow, become deep-sea sediments. They form layers of muddy ooze that can be up to 450 metres thick.

Most creatures that live on the seafloor are scavengers. A dead whale can provide food for millions of other animals, including shrimp-like amphipods and copepods, worms, rattails and hagfish.

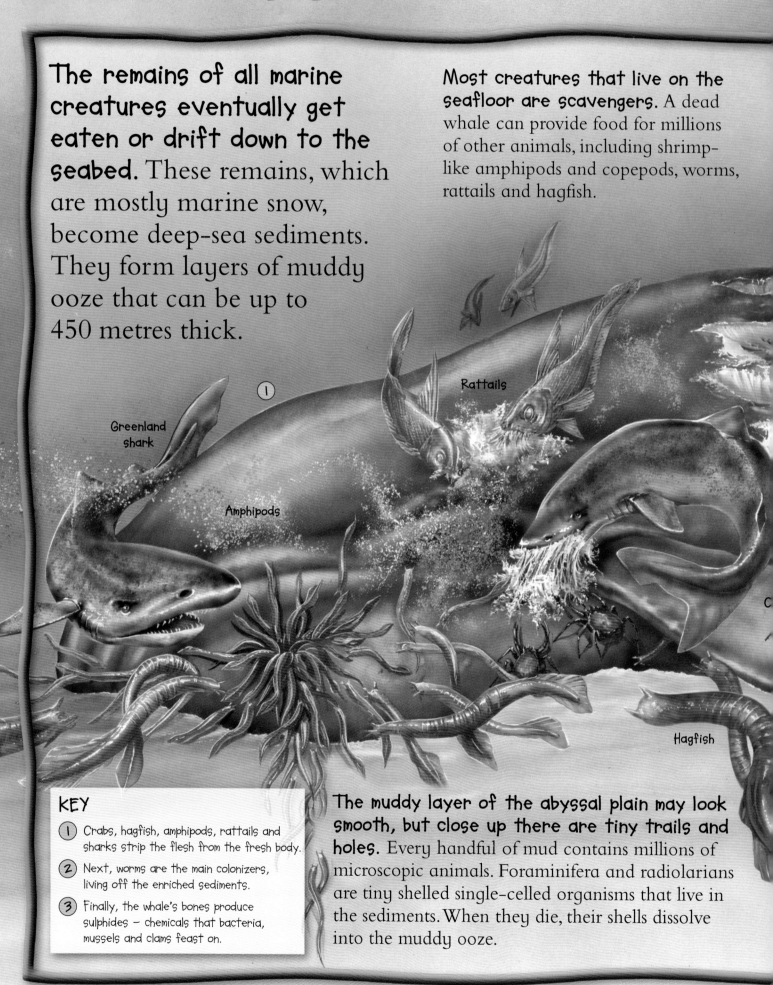

Greenland shark

Rattails

Amphipods

Hagfish

KEY
1. Crabs, hagfish, amphipods, rattails and sharks strip the flesh from the fresh body.
2. Next, worms are the main colonizers, living off the enriched sediments.
3. Finally, the whale's bones produce sulphides – chemicals that bacteria, mussels and clams feast on.

The muddy layer of the abyssal plain may look smooth, but close up there are tiny trails and holes. Every handful of mud contains millions of microscopic animals. Foraminifera and radiolarians are tiny shelled single-celled organisms that live in the sediments. When they die, their shells dissolve into the muddy ooze.

The abyssal plains are home to many types of sea cucumbers. These sausage-shaped animals are common in this habitat. Some burrow in the mud, while others can swim. Most move over the seafloor, picking up any bits of food they can find.

▼ It can take up to 100 years for a whale carcass to be devoured. More than 30,000 different types of animal feed and live off the carcass at different stages.

Mussels and clams

③

Bacterial mat

②

Squat lobster

Polychaete worms

I DON'T BELIEVE IT!

The seabed of the Antarctic Ocean has some mega-sized animals. Scientists found giant spiders and worms, and fish with huge eyes and body parts that scientists described as 'dangly bits'!

▼ Tripod fish stand still for hours at a time, facing the water currents, and wait for food to drift towards them.

Tripod fish have very long spines, called rays, on their fins. They use these to stand on the muddy seabed without sinking as they wait for prey to drift by. They are almost blind but can sense vibrations made by other animals nearby.

Deep heat

The deep ocean floor is mainly a cold place, where animals struggle to survive. However, there are some extraordinary areas where the water is heated to temperatures of 400°C and living things thrive.

▼ The minerals in the water produce dark clouds that look like smoke, and these vents are called 'black smokers'. Over time, they build up rocky structures called chimneys, which can grow to the height of a 15-storey building.

Below the Earth's surface is a layer of hot, semi-liquid rock, called magma. In places, magma is close to the ocean floor. Water seeps into cracks in rocks, called hydrothermal vents, and is heated. The water dissolves minerals from the rocks as it travels up towards the ocean floor, and bursts through a vent like a fountain.

The first hydrothermal vents were discovered in the Pacific Ocean in the 1970s. Since then, others have been found in the Atlantic, Indian and Arctic Oceans. The largest known region of hydrothermal vents lies near the Mid-Atlantic Ridge and is the size of a football pitch.

KEY
1. Vent mussel
2. Ratfish
3. Vent crab
4. Vent octopus
5. Chimney
6. Sea spider
7. Tube worms

Some hydrothermal vents do not support much life, other than microscopic creatures. Others support colonies of limpets, shrimps, starfish and tube worms, which survive without any sunlight. They are able to live and grow due to the minerals in the super-heated water from the vents.

▲ Hydrothermal vents known as 'white smokers' release cooler water and plumes of different minerals to black smokers.

Vent tube worms can grow to 2 metres long and they live without eating anything. Each worm is attached to the seabed and is protected by the tube it lives in. A red plume at the top collects seawater, which is rich in minerals. These minerals are passed to bacteria in the worm's body, and are then turned into nutrients.

Plume

Blood vessel

◄ Bacteria that live inside the tube worm turn the minerals into food, which the worm needs to survive.

Heart

Tube

Bacteria

UNDER PRESSURE

You will need:
milk carton   sticky tape

With an adult's help, make four holes on one side of an old milk carton, one above the other. Put sticky tape over the holes and fill the carton with water. Hold it over a bowl while you pull the tape off. Water will pour out fastest from the bottom hole because it has the most pressure on it.

Deep-sea coral

Tiny creatures called coral polyps build large reefs in the cold, deep ocean. Coral reefs are often found in warm, shallow waters, and they attract a wide variety of life. Cold-water reefs are less varied habitats, but there may be more cold-water reefs than warm-water ones.

Coral polyps have tube-shaped bodies and tentacles around their mouths. All polyps feed by filtering food particles from the water, and they have thousands of tiny stingers to stun bigger prey.

I DON'T BELIEVE IT!

Air pollution from carbon dioxide causes the oceans to become more acidic. This stops polyps, especially cold-water ones, from being able to grow their stony skeletons.

Coral polyps produce a hard substance called calcium carbonate, which forms a protective cup around them. Over time, the stony cups collect and grow into a reef, held together by a cement of sand, mud and other particles.

Bubble gum coral

Flytrap anemone

Lophelia pertusa

Squat lobster

▲ A specimen of bamboo coral is carefully lifted from the deep sea in a collection box that is attached to a submersible.

▼ Cold-water coral creates a special habitat where other animals can live, find food and shelter. A group of living things that depend on one habitat like this is called an ecosystem.

A type of cold-water coral polyp called *Lophelia* is the most common reef builder in the Atlantic Ocean. One reef can cover 2000 square kilometres and is home to animals such as squat lobsters, long-legged crabs, and fish – especially babies called larvae.

Other cold-water communities have been found in the deep oceans. Engineers drilling for oil in the Gulf of Mexico found cold seeps (places where gases leak out of cracks in the rocks) and animal life thrived nearby. The gases are an energy source for bacteria that feed there. Animals that feed on the bacteria are in turn eaten by crabs, corals, worms and fish.

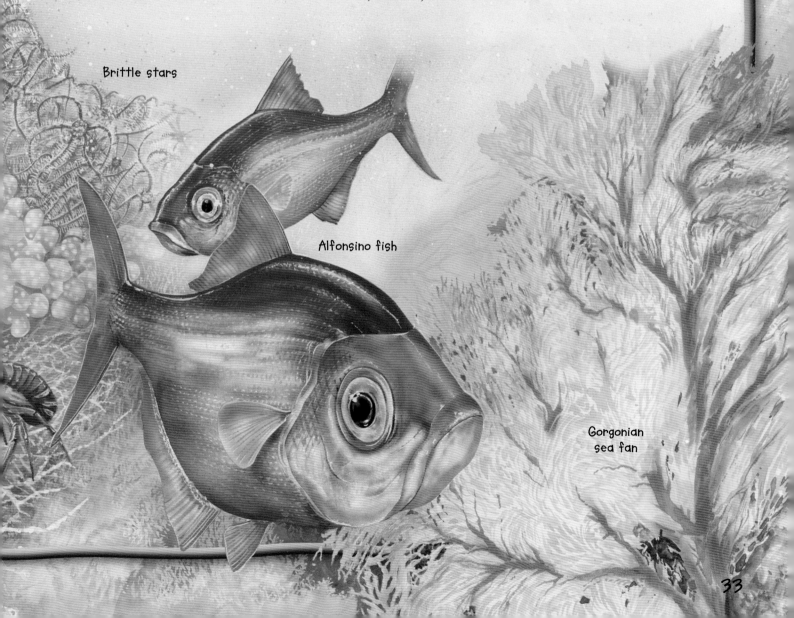

Brittle stars

Alfonsino fish

Gorgonian sea fan

On the move

Travelling in the ocean is different from travelling in air. Animals can simply float or drift along because they weigh 50 times less in water than they do in air. Currents help too. They can bring food to animals that are attached to the seabed, or they can carry animals towards food.

◀ Little sea butterflies are a type of sea snail. They can swim slowly through the water by flapping their 'wings', or they float in the currents.

▼ For this tube anemone, being attached to the seabed means it is impossible to make a quick getaway from the giant nudibranch that is attacking it (bottom).

Animals caught in deep-sea currents have to go with the flow, unless they are strong swimmers. Swimming takes 830 times as much energy as staying still because water is dense and heavy. Tiny zooplankton are weak swimmers, so when they get caught in currents, they drift along until they become free.

Many marine animals cannot move from one place to another. They are attached to the seabed and stay there, waiting for food to come to them. These animals, such as sea lilies and tube anemones, have feathery tentacles that they use to filter the seawater and collect particles of food.

Billions of animals undertake a journey every night. They travel up from the Twilight and Dark Zones into the Light Zone to feed, and return to deeper water in the morning. This mass movement is called a vertical migration and it represents the largest migration, or animal journey, on Earth.

Lantern fish are mighty movers of the ocean. The champion is called *Ceratoscopelus warmingii* and it lives at a depth of 1800 metres in the day. At night it swims upwards to depths of 100 metres to feed and avoid predators, and then it swims back. This feat is like a person running three marathons in a day!

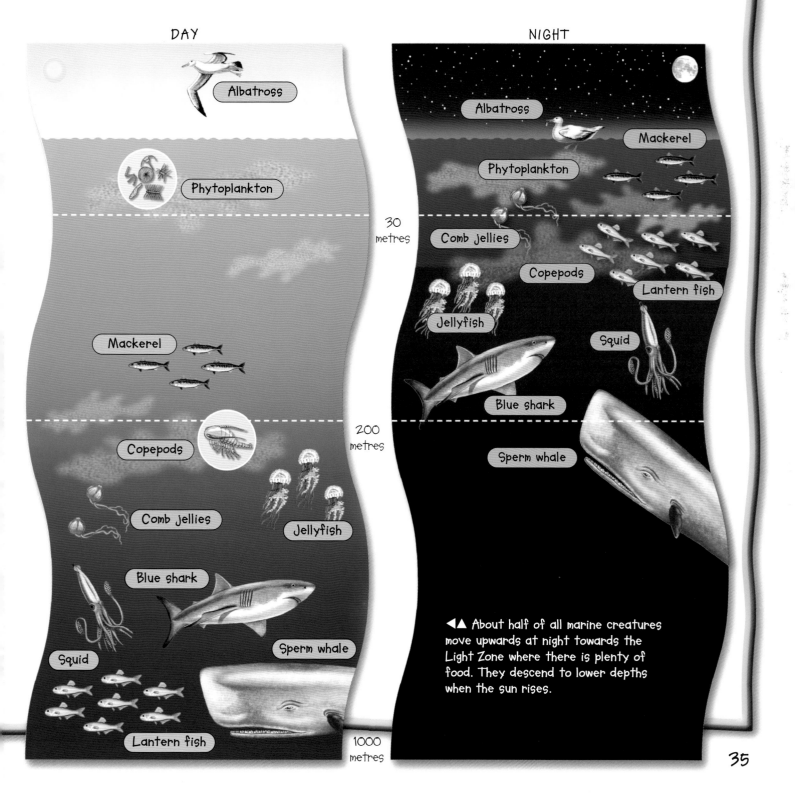

DAY

NIGHT

Albatross

Albatross

Mackerel

Phytoplankton

Phytoplankton

30 metres

Comb jellies

Copepods

Lantern fish

Jellyfish

Mackerel

Squid

Copepods

Blue shark

200 metres

Comb jellies

Jellyfish

Sperm whale

Blue shark

Squid

Sperm whale

◀▲ About half of all marine creatures move upwards at night towards the Light Zone where there is plenty of food. They descend to lower depths when the sun rises.

Lantern fish

1000 metres

Breathing and diving

Animals need to take a gas called oxygen into their bodies to release energy from food. Taking in oxygen is called breathing, and the process of using it to release energy is called respiration. Most marine animals are specially adapted to take in dissolved oxygen from seawater.

▲ As a shark swims, water enters its mouth, passes over its gills where oxygen is absorbed, and then leaves through the gill slits.

MAKE A SWIM BLADDER

Blow up a balloon. It is now filled with gas, like a swim bladder. Put the balloon in a bowl or bath of water and try to make it sink. Now fill the balloon with water, and see if it will float.

Fish breathe using gills. Like our lungs take oxygen from air, gills take in oxygen from water. Most fish also have a swim bladder, which helps them to cope with the changing pressure as they swim deeper. A swim bladder is a gas-filled sac that expands as a fish moves upwards, and shrinks as it descends. All deep-sea fish have gills, but they do not have swim bladders because the immense pressure would crush them.

Blowhole

◄ Whales, such as this killer whale, come to the surface to breathe. They have one or two blowholes on the top of their heads. These are like nostrils, and this is where air enters the body. When air is breathed out of a blowhole it creates a water spout.

As a sperm whale dives, its ribs and lungs contract (shrink). They expand again when the whale surfaces.

The whale's heartbeat slows by half so less oxygen is needed.

The spermaceti organ is a huge mass of oil. It probably helps the whale to dive deep by changing its ability to float.

The nasal passages fill with cool water to help the whale sink.

▲ The sperm whale is adapted for diving in very deep water. It can stay underwater for up to 90 minutes while hunting for giant squid.

Seals, dolphins and whales are air-breathing mammals, but their bodies are adapted to life in water. The sperm whale can store oxygen in its blood and muscles, which allows it to descend to over 1000 metres to hunt. Its flexible ribcage allows the whale's lungs to shrink during a dive.

Super-speedy pilot whales are called 'cheetahs of the deep'. During the day, these predators swim at depths of around 300 metres, but at night they plunge to 1000 metres in search of prey. Pilot whales can plummet 9 metres a second at top swimming speed. They need to be fast to catch their prey of large squid, but also because they need to get back to the surface to breathe.

▼ Most marine worms have feathery gills that absorb oxygen from the water. However, some do not have gills and absorb oxygen through their skin.

Simple creatures do not have special body parts for breathing. They can absorb oxygen from the water directly through their skins. The amount of oxygen in the water falls from the surface to a depth of around 1000 metres, but it increases again at greater depths.

Glow in the dark

Animals of the deep create their own light to attract prey, a mate or to confuse predators. This is called bioluminescence and it takes place in organs called photophores. These usually produce blue light, but some animals can glow with green, red or yellow light.

Bioluminescent lure used to attract prey

Under white light

◀ A shortnose greeneye fish produces its own light. In the dark, it glows green, especially its eyes.

In the dark

▶ The special cells inside a photophore that produce light are called photocytes.

Light rays

Skin

Lens

Colour filter

Photocytes (light-producing cells)

Reflector

Hatchet fish are deceivers of the Twilight Zone. Photophores on their bellies produce light and disguise the fishes' outlines when seen from below, against the faint light. Hatchet fish can also adjust the light to match the brightness of any light from above.

◀ The viperfish has rows of photophores along its underside. These help to hide it from predators below.

Spotted lantern fish use their photophores to attract mates. They are one of the brightest deep-sea fish, with brilliant displays of bioluminescence along their sides and bellies. The photophores are arranged in different patterns depending on whether the fish is male or female, and what type of lantern fish it is. This helps the fish to find the right mate.

It is not just fish that can glow in the dark. Mauve stinger jellyfish emit a beautiful violet-blue colour when they are disturbed. Firefly squid not only cover their bodies with lights, they can also produce a cloud of glowing particles that distracts predators while they make a quick getaway.

▶ Mauve stinger jellyfish produce quick flashes of light when they sense movement in the water. They even flash when waves pass over them at the ocean's surface.

Tiny vampire squid have enormous eyes and can produce light all over their bodies whenever they want to. These squid are able to control their bioluminescence, producing dazzling displays of patterned light that can be dimmed or brightened, probably to scare off predators. When a vampire squid is hunting it does not light up. This means it can surprise its prey.

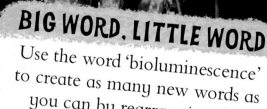

BIG WORD, LITTLE WORD
Use the word 'bioluminescence' to create as many new words as you can by rearranging the letters. Each word must be at least two letters long. Use a dictionary to check the spelling of your words.

39

Deep-sea food

The ocean food chain begins in the Light Zone. Phytoplankton use the Sun's energy to grow. In turn, they are eaten by other creatures, passing on energy and nutrients. It takes a long time for energy and nutrients to filter down to the sea floor, so many deep-sea animals scavenge food, eating whatever they find, while others hunt.

▼ Nearly all energy used by marine life comes from the Light Zone. Phytoplankton begin the nutrient cycle, and upward-flowing water currents complete it by bringing nutrients back to the surface.

Sun

Phytoplankton

Zooplankton

Upwelling of nutrients

Carnivores

Faeces and animal remains fall as marine snow

Bacteria and bottom feeders such a sea cucumbers process marine snow, releasing nutrients

Copepods and krill (zooplankton) may be small but they play a big role in the deep-ocean ecosystem. These tiny, plant-eating crustaceans exist in their billions. They swim up to the surface every evening to try to avoid being eaten. In the morning they swim back down into the deep, dark waters. Krill can live to depths of 2000 metres.

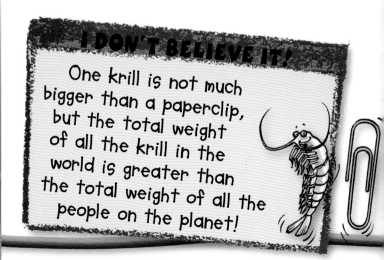

I DON'T BELIEVE IT!

One krill is not much bigger than a paperclip, but the total weight of all the krill in the world is greater than the total weight of all the people on the planet!

◀ Goblin sharks have soft, flabby bodies and long, strange-looking snouts. They are pinkish white in colour.

Large predators, such as sharks, seals and whales, may reach the Dark Zone, but few go deeper. Goblin sharks swim slowly in the Dark Zone and they have snouts that may help them to find food. Their huge jaws can snap forwards to grab prey such as small fish and squid.

▼ Gulper eels can grown to 2 metres in length. They have pink photophores on their tails to attract prey.

Fangtooth fish are also known as ogrefish. They use their unusually sharp, long teeth to grab hold of squid and fish. Food is scarce in the deep ocean, but with such large jaws, fangtooths attempt to eat almost any prey that comes along, even animals that are larger than themselves.

▶ This soft-bodied animal called a predatory tunicate lives in the Twlight Zone. When an animal swims into its hood-like mouth it closes shut like a Venus flytrap.

Gulper eels are all mouth. These predators of the Dark Zone have enormous mouths, but small teeth. It may be that gulper eels use their big mouths for catching lots of small prey at a time, rather than one large, meaty prey.

Anglerfish

If you cannot find food in the dark, make it come to you! Anglerfish have long growths on their heads that work like fishing rods, and the tips are coated in glowing bacteria. Other animals are attracted to the glowing light, called a lure, and are quickly snapped up by the anglerfish.

▲ In the 2003 Disney Pixar movie *Finding Nemo*, Marlin and Dory narrowly escape the jaws of an anglerfish.

There are many different types of anglerfish and all look very strange. The hairy anglerfish is one of the strangest and it lives at depths of up to 1500 metres. It gets its name from its fins, which have long spikes, and the sensitive hairs that cover its body.

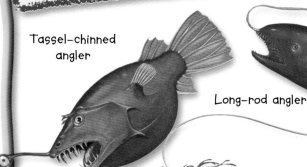

Tassel-chinned angler

Long-rod angler

Deep-sea angler

Males

▶ Two tiny males are attached to this female Regan's anglerfish. These anglerfish are sometimes called phantom anglerfish.

Finding a mate in the dark can be tough, so some male anglerfish stay attached to a female! The males are much smaller than the females, so they can grab hold and hitch a lift that lasts for life. While scientists have found many types of female anglerfish they are still searching for some of their tiny male relations!

A dragonfish also lures prey to its death. When a dragonfish spies a shrimp to eat it produces a red spotlight made by photophores below its eyes. The shrimp can't see red, so it is unaware it is being hunted. The dragonfish then snaps up its prey in its large mouth, full of ultra-sharp teeth.

▼ Monkfish are so well camouflaged that they are almost impossible to spot when lying on the ocean floor.

Anglers are types of anglerfish that lie on the seafloor. Their wide, flat bodies are covered in soft, fleshy growths that help them to blend in with the mud where they hide. Anglers use their fins to shuffle along, flicking their lures as they go. They are often caught and sold as food, and also better known as monkfish.

Hide and seek

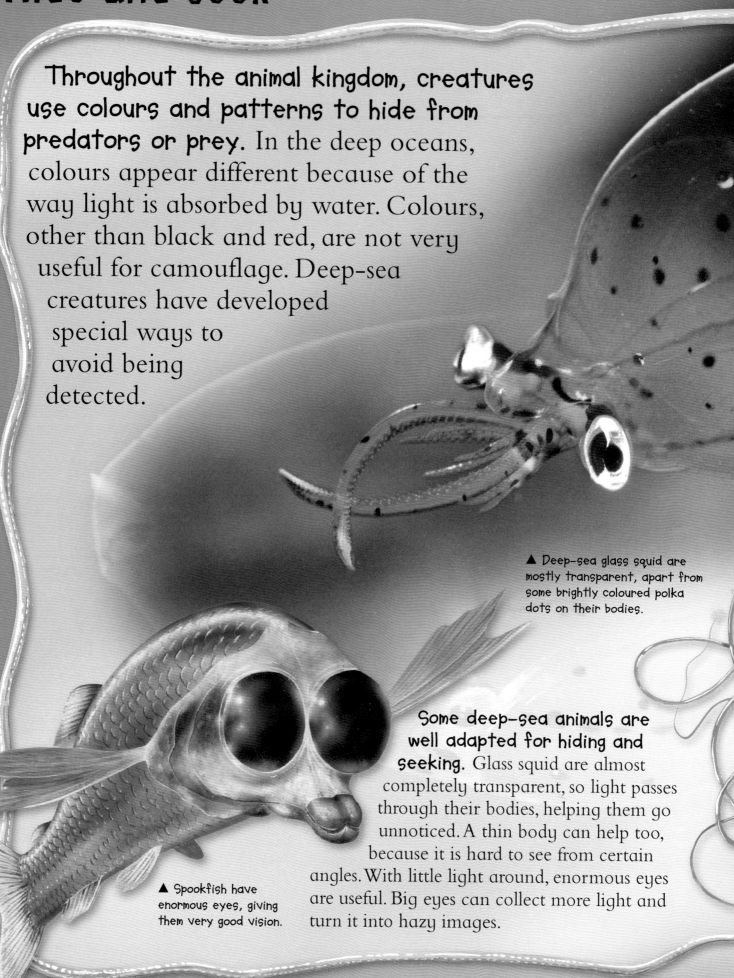

Throughout the animal kingdom, creatures use colours and patterns to hide from predators or prey. In the deep oceans, colours appear different because of the way light is absorbed by water. Colours, other than black and red, are not very useful for camouflage. Deep-sea creatures have developed special ways to avoid being detected.

▲ Deep-sea glass squid are mostly transparent, apart from some brightly coloured polka dots on their bodies.

▲ Spookfish have enormous eyes, giving them very good vision.

Some deep-sea animals are well adapted for hiding and seeking. Glass squid are almost completely transparent, so light passes through their bodies, helping them go unnoticed. A thin body can help too, because it is hard to see from certain angles. With little light around, enormous eyes are useful. Big eyes can collect more light and turn it into hazy images.

Silvery scales on a fish's back are perfect for reflecting light and confusing a predator. When shimmering scales are seen against dim rays of light in the Twilight Zone, the outline of a fish's body becomes less obvious, and it fades into the background or even disappears.

When there is no light, animals rely on senses other than sight. Many deep-sea animals can feel vibrations in the water. Shrimp have sensory organs all over their bodies, including their antennae, which can detect movements nearby. Many fish can also sense the small electrical fields generated by other living things.

Silvery, reflective scales

Light-producing photophores

▲ By using their photophores to produce light and their silvery scales to reflect light, hatchet fish become almost invisible to predators.

► The snipe eel's jaws curve away from each other so they never fully close.

Snipe eels have long, ribbon-like bodies, and jaws that look like a bird's bill. They live at depths of up to 1800 metres and can grown to 1.5 metres in length. As males mature their jaws shrink, but their nostrils grow longer. This probably improves their sense of smell and helps them to find females.

ODD ONE OUT

Which of these animals uses colour and pattern to scare other animals, rather than to hide?
Zebra   Wasp   Tiger
Leaf insect
Arctic fox

Answer:
Wasp

45

CORAL REEF

Beautiful coral reefs lie beneath the sparkling surfaces of sapphire-blue seas. Although they only take up a tiny amount of space in the world's oceans, coral reefs contain more than one-quarter of all types of sea creatures and are home to billions of animals and plants. Coral reefs are among the Earth's most precious places but they are in grave danger of disappearing forever.

◀ Reefs teem with life as fish dart and dash around stone-like coral structures. Panda butterflyfish inhabit reefs in tropical oceans and can grow up to 20 centimetres in length.

What are coral reefs?

Coral reefs are ocean habitats (homes) made by the creatures that live inside them. Tiny coral animals called polyps live together in huge numbers, known as colonies. They can grow for thousands of years, building reefs that can measure more than 2000 kilometres long.

▲ The coral reefs in the Florida Keys National Marine Sanctuary are so vast they can be seen from space.

Reefs are home to many animals and plants. Together, the reef and all the things living in it make up an ecosystem. Coral reefs are some of the most varied ecosystems in the world, and are thriving, colourful places that burst with life.

◀ Sea anemones attach themselves to the reef structure and fish hide away in the many nooks and crannies.

CORAL REEF KEY

1. White-spotted rose anemone
2. Club-tipped anemone
3. Gopher rockfish

It is not only coral polyps that help a reef to grow. Polyps provide the framework of a reef, but other living things add to the structure. Some marine (sea) organisms, such as sponges and sea cucumbers, have a hard substance called silicon in their skeletons. When they die, their skeletons add to the coral reef.

Land-living animals and plants also depend on reefs. In shallow water, plants take root in the mud and sand that collects around a reef. Mangrove trees and sea grasses grow here – the spaces around their roots make good places for animals, such as crabs, to hide. Long-legged birds also wade through mud and water, looking for food.

Coral reefs have been around for at least 230 million years. They are among the oldest ecosystems in the world. Despite their great age, coral reefs do not appear to have changed very much in this time.

◄ The warm waters around mangrove roots are a perfect place for soft tree corals to grow.

Coral animals

Coral polyps are the little animals that build reefs. Their soft bodies are like rubber tubes with an opening at their centre. This is the mouth, which is surrounded by rows of tentacles. Each tentacle is equipped with stingers called cnidocytes (say nido-sites).

Coral polyps have a special relationship with tiny life-forms called zooxanthellae (say zoo-zan-thell-ee). These are plant-like algae that live inside a polyp's body, providing it with some of the food it needs to grow. In return, the polyps provide the algae with a safe place to live. Zooxanthellae need sunlight to survive, so they live inside a polyp's tentacles, where light can reach them.

◄ Cup corals are a non reef-building species that use their tentacles to catch prey. Coral polyps are in the same animal family as jellyfish and sea anemones, and are known as 'cnidarians' (say nid-air-ee-ans).

Sea animals do not always go looking for food. Coral polyps cannot move around, so they grab whatever food comes their way, using their tentacles. When a tentacle touches something edible, a tiny stinger springs out and pierces the prey's skin. The tentacles draw the prey into the polyp's mouth.

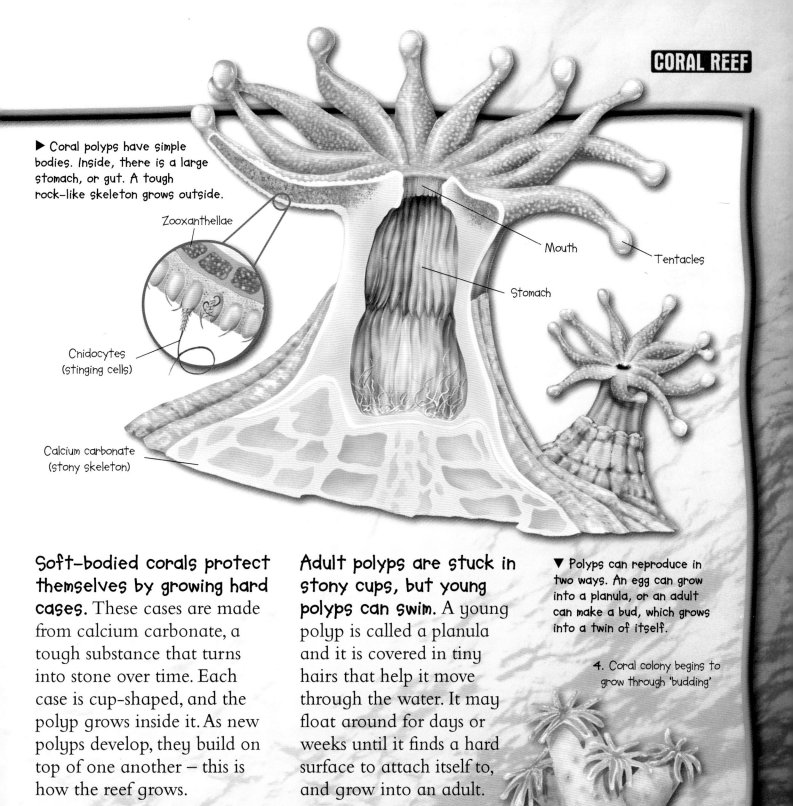

▶ Coral polyps have simple bodies. Inside, there is a large stomach, or gut. A tough rock-like skeleton grows outside.

Zooxanthellae

Chnidocytes (stinging cells)

Calcium carbonate (stony skeleton)

Mouth

Stomach

Tentacles

Soft-bodied corals protect themselves by growing hard cases. These cases are made from calcium carbonate, a tough substance that turns into stone over time. Each case is cup-shaped, and the polyp grows inside it. As new polyps develop, they build on top of one another – this is how the reef grows.

Adult polyps are stuck in stony cups, but young polyps can swim. A young polyp is called a planula and it is covered in tiny hairs that help it move through the water. It may float around for days or weeks until it finds a hard surface to attach itself to, and grow into an adult.

▼ Polyps can reproduce in two ways. An egg can grow into a planula, or an adult can make a bud, which grows into a twin of itself.

4. Coral colony begins to grow through 'budding'

1. Planula searches for a place to settle

3. Polyp begins to grow a stony cup

2. Planula attaches to a hard surface

51

Hard and soft

There are two main types of coral – hard coral and soft coral. Hard coral polyps are reef-builders – they use calcium carbonate to build strong structures around themselves. Soft corals are bendy, and often live alongside their stony cousins.

Warm water reefs can look like colourful gardens. Corals grow in many unusual shapes, appearing like bushes, trees and mushrooms. The shape of coral depends upon the type of polyp that lives within it, and its position on the reef.

Some corals are easy to identify because they look just like their name. Brain corals, for example, look like brains. They grow very slowly and can reach the size of a boulder. Staghorn coral is one of the fastest-growing types, and it is an important reef-builder, especially in shallow waters. Each staghorn polyp can live for around ten years, and will not reproduce until it reaches at least three years old.

▼ Corals are different shapes and sizes. The way each coral grows depends on the type of polyps that live inside the rocky structures.

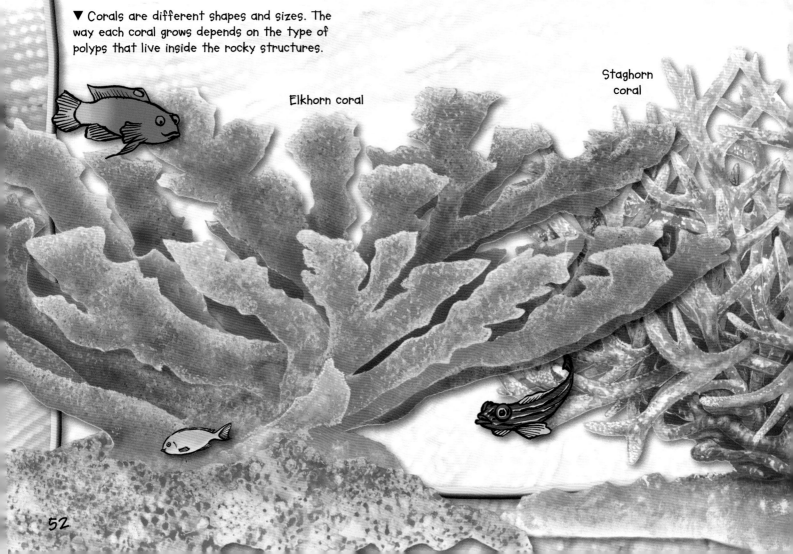

Elkhorn coral

Staghorn coral

Brain
coral

Mushroom
coral

Not all coral polyps live together in colonies. Some types live alone in the Southern Ocean, near the Antarctic, where temperatures rarely creep above a chilly 6°C. Little is known about solitary corals, but it is thought they are sensitive to water temperature.

Lettuce
coral

Sea fan

Sea whip

Soft tree coral

53

Where in the world?

Warm water coral reefs may be packed with life, but they only cover around 284,000 square kilometres of the Earth's surface. If you put them all together, they would still only take up the same room as a small country, such as New Zealand.

Coral polyps are choosy about where they grow. This is because the zooxanthellae that live with them need warmth and light to turn the sun's energy into food. They are most likely to grow in seas and oceans within a region called the tropics, which is between the Tropic of Cancer and the Tropic of Capricorn.

◄ Damselfish and sea anemones are just two of the many animals that live on the Indian Ocean reefs.

--- Tropic of Cancer ---

RED SEA

▲ Blue-spotted stingrays hunt their prey among the Red Sea corals.

Coral Triangle

--- Equator ---

INDIAN OCEAN

The Coral Triangle is an enormous region that stretches across the seas around Indonesia, Malaysia and Papua New Guinea. It contains some of the world's most precious reefs, and is home to 3000 species of fish and 20 species of mammals, including dugongs, whales and dolphins.

--- Tropic of Capricorn ---

◄ A pink porcelain crab rests on a hard coral near Malaysia, in the Coral Triangle.

Dirty water is no good to coral polyps. They prefer clear water, without the tiny particles of dirt, mud or sand that prevent light from reaching the seabed. Reefs don't grow near river mouths, or in areas where dirt is washed from the land into the sea. Polyps are even fussy about the amount of salt dissolved in the ocean water around them.

◀ Pygmy seahorses live in the warm coral waters of the western Pacific Ocean.

◀ The Hawaiian reef fish Humuhumunukunukuapua'a is a type of triggerfish, and makes pig-like snorting sounds if threatened.

ATLANTIC OCEAN

Hawaiian reefs

PACIFIC OCEAN

CARIBBEAN SEA

Mesoamerican Reef

Sunlight cannot pass through water as easily as it can pass through air. As zooxanthellae need light, their coral polyps only grow in water with a maximum depth of around 11 metres – although this varies depending on how clean the water is. This explains why warm water coral reefs grow near the land, where the water is shallow.

▲ The Caribbean reef octopus feeds at night, and eats fish and shelled animals.

CORAL SEA

◀ Giant clams live in coral reefs around the South Pacific and Indian Oceans.

SOUTHERN OCEAN

Types of reef

There are three main types of coral reef. Fringing reefs are the most common. They grow on the edges of land that are underwater, often with little or no gap in between the reef and dry land. Barrier reefs also grow where land meets the ocean, but they are separated from the land by a stretch of water, called a lagoon. Atolls are circular reefs with a lagoon in the centre.

1 When coral grows around an island's coasts, a fringing reef develops.

Island   Reef

For a long time, no one knew how atoll reefs formed. The scientist Charles Darwin (1809–1882) suggested that most atolls had grown on the edges of islands or volcanoes that had since disappeared. He thought the islands might have sunk into the sea, but the reefs kept growing. In 1953, Darwin's theory was proved right.

2 The island drops, or the sea rises, and the coral becomes a barrier reef.

Island   Lagoon   Reef

Patch reefs form in shallow water and their tops are only visible at low tide. They are usually round or oval in shape and their outer edges are ringed by coral sand leading to beds of sea grass.

Bank reefs often grow in lines, or in semi-circles. They have large buttress zones (the area of a reef that faces the sea) with ridges of tough coral that grow out into it. Elkhorn coral grows here because it is able to withstand strong waves.

The Maldives are coral islands in the Indian Ocean. As they are built from coral, most land is no more than 1.5 metres above sea level. People have been living in the Maldives for more than 2000 years. There is little soil on the islands so few plants, other than coconut palms, grow well. Local people have survived by fishing and, more recently from tourism.

③ When there is no longer any sign of the island the reef is called an atoll.

Reef   Lagoon

Zones of the reef

Coral reefs can grow so large that it is possible to see them from outer space. Yet it is only the outer parts of a reef that are alive. The parts beneath the surface are dead, made up from the billions of stony cups that once housed living coral polyps.

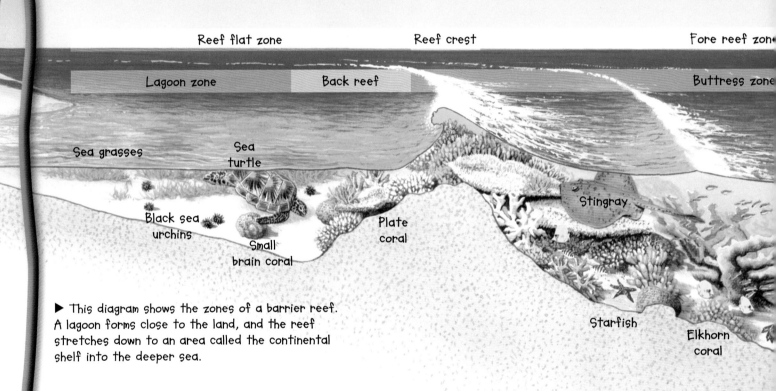

Reef flat zone — Reef crest — Fore reef zone

Lagoon zone — Back reef — Buttress zone

Sea grasses — Sea turtle — Black sea urchins — Small brain coral — Plate coral — Stingray — Starfish — Elkhorn coral

▶ This diagram shows the zones of a barrier reef. A lagoon forms close to the land, and the reef stretches down to an area called the continental shelf into the deeper sea.

The part of a reef that is closest to land is called a reef flat. It is difficult for polyps to grow well here because of the effect of the tides, which may leave the coral exposed to air for too long, and because the water can become too salty. The reef flat is home to many types of animals that scuttle around between sea grasses, dig into the soft mud, or stick to the old, dead stony structures.

Most corals grow on the sides of the reef that face the sea and wind. This area is known as the fore reef and it is warmed by ocean currents. The corals here grow upwards and outwards, building up layers over thousands of years. Below the fore reef is a collection of old coral material that has broken off and fallen to the seafloor. The highest part of the fore reef is the crest — the polyps that live here must be able to survive strong waves and winds.

The fore reef is divided into three parts. At the bottom, plate-shaped corals grow where there is less light. As they grow they spread out to reach the sunlight. Nearby, fan corals are stretched in front of the water currents that flow towards them. In the middle part larger, mound-shaped corals grow and near the crest, long-fingered strong corals, such as staghorn, appear.

Further out to sea, a reef develops a buttress zone. Here, large spurs or clumps of coral grow, breaking up the waves and absorbing some of their impact before they hit the rest of the reef. This is the area where sharks and barracudas are most likely to swim. Beyond the buttress zone lies the reef wall, which forms in a deeper part of the sea.

Deep reef zone

Bottlenose dolphins

Sea goldies

Sea whip

Sea fan

Maze coral

Tube sponge

Butterfly fish

Dead coral bedrock

Lettuce coral

Star coral

Wobbegong shark

Barracudas

Whitetip reef shark

I DON'T BELIEVE IT!

Coral reefs are very slow growers. A reef can grow about 10 centimetres a year if the conditions are just right – how much have you grown in the last year?

59

Cold water corals

In the cold, dark ocean waters, coral reefs lay hidden for thousands of years. A few of these deep sea reefs were found about 250 years ago, but it has recently been discovered that in fact, there are more cold water reefs than warm water ones.

BIG BUILDERS

Find out about some other animal architects. Use the Internet or the library to discover how bees, termites and sociable weaver birds work together to build structures.

Cold water corals live in waters between 200 and 1500 metres deep. The largest cold water coral reef is more than 40 kilometres long and up to 3 kilometres wide. Just like warm water corals, these deep sea reefs are home to a large range of animals, many of which live nowhere else on Earth.

▼ A cold water reef grows in the chilly waters north of Scotland. Visible are dead man's fingers coral (1), a jewel anemone (2) and a common sea urchin (3).

Deep sea coral polyps don't have zooxanthellae, so they don't need sunlight to survive. They have to get all their food by feeding on tiny animals, called zooplankton, that drift past them. They catch these creatures with their tentacles and poison stingers, and draw them into their mouths.

◄ Zooplankton are tiny, shrimp-like animals eaten by cold water corals brought to them on strong water currents.

Cold water corals take thousands of years to grow, but they are being destroyed at an alarming rate. Scientists believe most of the damage is caused by trawling, a type of fishing. A heavy net is pulled over, or near, the sea floor by a boat. As it is dragged along the net catches fish, but it also damages coral and churns up mud and pollution.

The white coral *Lophelia pertusa* is a stony cold water coral responsible for most of the reefs in the Atlantic Ocean. Scientists have discovered more than 1300 species of animal living on one group of reefs in the cold North Atlantic Ocean. The reefs are home to many animals, including sharks, crabs, sponges, conger eels, snails and worms.

▼ Wolf-fish have powerful jaws, which they use to eat crabs and shelled animals that live around cold water corals.

The Great Barrier Reef

The Great Barrier Reef, on the north-east coast of Australia, is possibly the largest structure ever built by animals. It covers an area of the Coral Sea that extends for more than 2000 kilometres and it took around 18 million years for the reef to grow to this enormous size.

It may look like one giant structure, but the Great Barrier Reef is really made up of around 3000 smaller reefs and 1000 islands. Although coral has grown in this region for millions of years the barrier reef only formed at the end of the last Ice Age, around 10,000 years ago.

The Great Barrier Reef was not studied by scientists until the 18th century. British explorer James Cook (1728–1779) sailed his ship, HMS *Endeavour*, onto the reef in June 1770, and his crew had to spend six weeks repairing the damage to their craft. Ever since, explorers and scientists have been studying the structure of the reef and its wildlife.

◄ When leafy seadragons hide among seaweed they become almost invisible.

▼ Dugongs are air-breathing animals that swim around the reef, grazing on sea grasses.

In 1975, the Great Barrier Reef Marine Park was set up to protect the reef. The area is home to an enormous variety of living things – there are 5000 species of molluscs, 1500 species of fish, 400 species of coral, 200 species of birds, 125 species of sharks, rays and skates, 30 species of whales, dolphins and porpoises, 14 species of sea snakes and six species of marine turtles!

▶ Groups, or shoals, of sweetlips swim around the Great Barrier Reef.

QUIZ

Can you add up all the numbers of species listed in fact 144, from molluscs to turtles? Check your answer with a calculator.

Answer:
5000 + 1500 + 400 + 200 +125 + 30 + 14 + 6 = 7275.

Native people and nearby islanders from the Torres Strait have fished in the Coral Sea for more than 60,000 years. They are known as the Traditional Owners of the Great Barrier Reef. The areas of the reef that they used in the practice of their ancient lifestyles are called the sea country. Traditional Owners work to preserve their ancient connection to the Great Barrier Reef.

◀ Like many sea snakes, olive sea snakes have a poisonous bite.

Caribbean coral

The world's second largest coral reef protects people from the effects of hurricanes (violent storms). It is called the Mesoamerican Reef, and it lies in the Caribbean Sea, west of the Atlantic Ocean.

Large areas of mangrove forest grow at the land's edge, behind the reef. Together, the mangroves and the corals create a barrier that slows down the hurricane-force storms that often batter the Caribbean coastlines. Mangrove roots help to bind the fragile shoreline, and stop rain and river water from washing too much dirt towards the coral. They also act as nurseries for young reef fish.

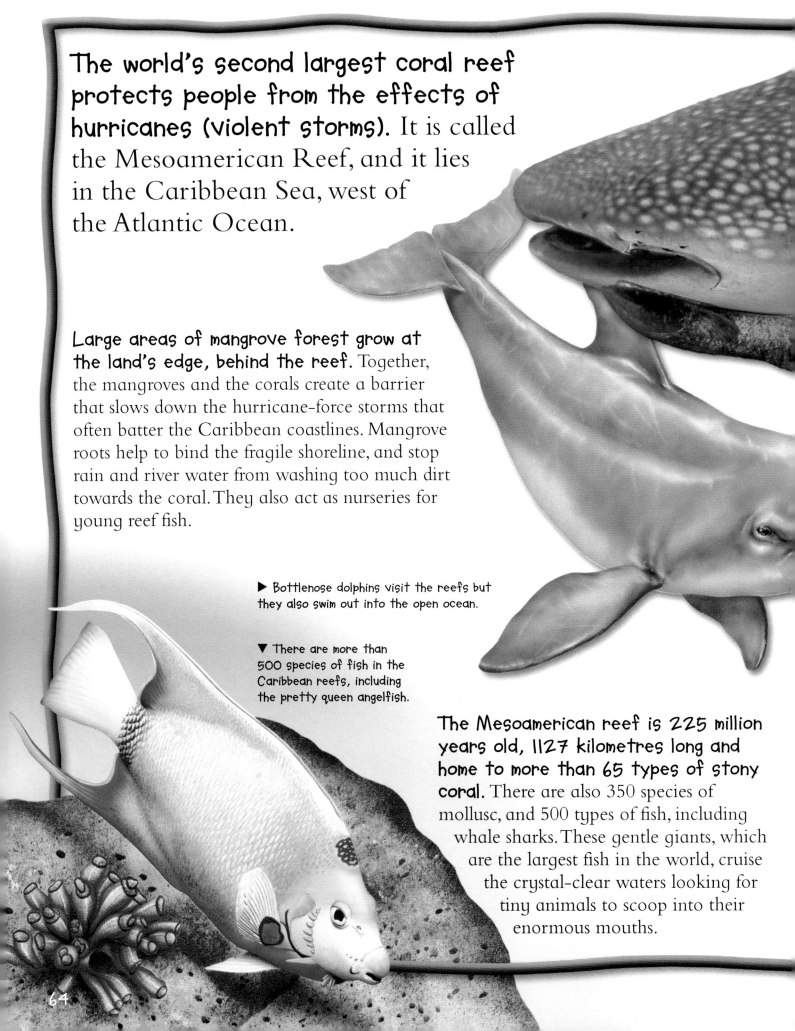

▶ Bottlenose dolphins visit the reefs but they also swim out into the open ocean.

▼ There are more than 500 species of fish in the Caribbean reefs, including the pretty queen angelfish.

The Mesoamerican reef is 225 million years old, 1127 kilometres long and home to more than 65 types of stony coral. There are also 350 species of mollusc, and 500 types of fish, including whale sharks. These gentle giants, which are the largest fish in the world, cruise the crystal-clear waters looking for tiny animals to scoop into their enormous mouths.

▲ It is thought that whale sharks can live to be 100 years old or more. They eat small fish and krill around reefs and in deep water.

X MARKS THE SPOT!
Create a treasure map for a coral island. Use old teabags to stain it and tear the edges of the paper to make it look old. Remember to mark the treasure's location with a big X.

Throughout history, people who live near the reef have depended on its fish for food. Many of the people who live in coastal areas in countries such as Belize, Mexico, Honduras and Guatemala have long family traditions of fishing around the reef. They discovered that swarms of fish come together during full moons to mate, and this was the perfect time to catch them in nets.

▲ Tourists enjoy the wildlife spectacle around a reef. They can snorkel, or take a ride in a glass-bottomed boat.

Pirates used to hide their ships among the many Caribbean islands that are dotted along the reef. Explorers came too, looking for treasure such as gold and silver, and to set up trading routes. Today, tourists flock to the area to enjoy exploring this ecosystem and its beautiful coral gardens.

Islands of fire

The coral reefs of Hawaii are unlike any others found on Earth. They have formed around a string of islands, called an archipelago, that developed when volcanoes erupted in the middle of the Pacific Ocean. Hawaii is about 3200 kilometres from any large land mass, which means these are the world's most isolated group of islands.

Around one-quarter of the animals and plants that live on Hawaiian coral reefs are found nowhere else. Algae, which are seaweeds, thrive in this area – especially the stony seaweeds that help to bind reefs together and make them stronger. Algae are important because they take carbon dioxide from the air and expel oxygen, the gas that animals such as polyps need to breathe.

▼ Enormous humpback whales use the waters around Hawaii as nurseries. They stay here with their young until it is time to swim north.

I DON'T BELIEVE IT!

Huge humpback whales feed on tiny krill, which are shrimp-like creatures. They don't feed in the winter, so at this time of year the krill have nothing to fear.

▲▶ Hawaiian corals (1) have grown on old lava that has cooled and turned to stone (2).

Volcanoes began to erupt in this area around 70 million years ago, and they are still active today. As lava cooled and turned to stone, corals began to grow on their edges. The first polyps must have arrived as free-swimming planulas, probably from other Pacific coral reefs.

Around 10,000 endangered humpback whales visit Hawaii every year. They arrive at the warm tropical waters in the winter, after swimming all the way from their feeding grounds in Alaska. While in Hawaii, the whales give birth to their young, and care for them. They can be seen swimming, playing and even battling with one another around the coral reefs.

◀ Green turtles lay their eggs on Hawaiian beaches because the reefs protect them from storms and waves.

The islanders of Hawaii set up a marine park in 1967, to protect the reef ecosystem. In 1956 an enormous channel, more than 60 metres wide, was blasted into the coral using dynamite to make way for a new telephone cable. The coral is now protected by law.

◀ A bobtail squid can produce light in its belly, which helps it hunt at night. The light is produced by bacteria that live on the squid.

A carnival of colour

Some animals stay on the sea floor, or hide in cracks in the coral reef, but others dart, dive and dazzle their way through the clear waters. Coral reef animals often use the colours of their shells or skins to help them lurk unseen in the shadows, or to warn other animals to stay away. When an animal uses colour to hide, it is said to be camouflaged.

Coral fish come in beautiful patterns and brilliant colours. Good looks are important for their survival – red colours appear dark in water, stripes provide camouflage and spots can confuse predators. Blue and yellow fish look bright to us, but they are hidden on the reef. The way sunlight is reflected off coral reefs affects the appearance of blues and yellows, making them blend in with the background.

▲▼ Coral fish come in many different colours and patterns such as the coral trout (top), regal angelfish (middle) and blue tang fish (below).

Squid and cuttlefish create flashes of colour. These soft-bodied molluscs can change their colours in an instant to hide or attract prey towards them. They can produce skin colours of red, yellow, orange, brown and black – and can even create patterns, such as zebra stripes, on their skin.

◄ Sea slugs are brightly coloured to warn predators that they are very poisonous.

Land slugs are slimy and often dull in colour, but coral reef slugs are bizarre, beautiful animals. Sea slugs, also called nudibranchs, don't have shells, but they do have soft, feathery gills on their backs, which help them to breathe in water. Some nudibranchs are small, but the largest ones can grow to 30 centimetres long.

The stripes, spines and bright colours of a lionfish spell danger to other coral creatures. These ocean fish hunt other fish, shrimp and sea anemones. When they are threatened they react with lightning speed. Lionfish have spines on their bodies that carry deadly venom, which they raise and plunge into a predator's flesh.

▼ Lionfish hide among rocks in the daytime, and only come out at night to hunt for food. They have been known to threaten divers.

GO FISH!

Choose your favourite colourful coral fish from this book and copy it onto a large piece of paper or card. Use different materials, such as paints, tissue paper, buttons and foil to show the colours and patterns.

On the attack

Animals need energy to survive, and they get that energy from food. Some reef animals graze on seaweeds and corals, but others hunt and kill to feed. Hunting animals are called predators, and their victims are called prey.

▶ When sharks, such as these lemon sharks, sense blood or food they move with speed to attack their prey.

Some coral sharks aren't aggressive and divers can feed them by hand. Bull sharks are not so relaxed around humans. They have been known to attack divers and swimmers around reefs. Sharks are drawn to coral reefs because of the thousands of fish on the reef but finding prey is not always easy when there are so many good hiding places.

Cone shells look harmless, but their appearance is deceptive. These sea snails crawl around reefs looking for prey such as worms, molluscs and fish. They fire venom-filled darts to paralyze their prey. The dart remains attached to the cone shell, so it can draw its victim back to its body and devour it.

◀ This small animal cannot protect itself from an attack by a deadly cone shell.

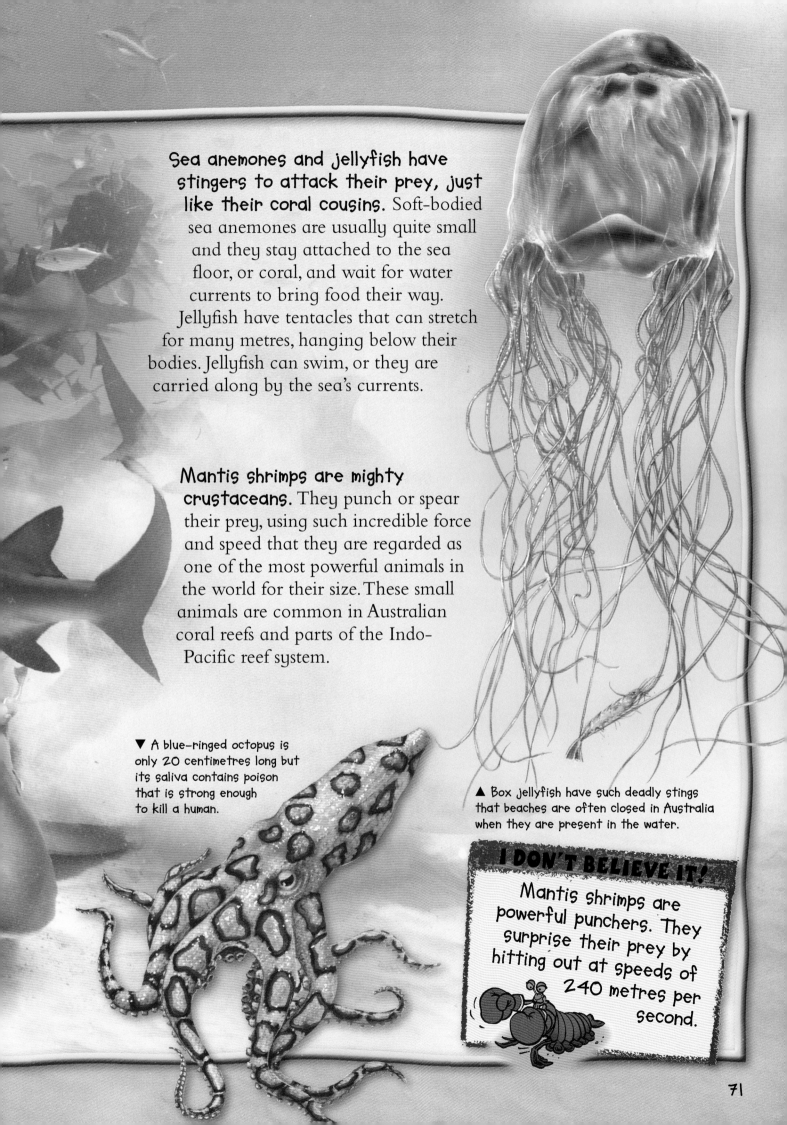

Sea anemones and jellyfish have stingers to attack their prey, just like their coral cousins. Soft-bodied sea anemones are usually quite small and they stay attached to the sea floor, or coral, and wait for water currents to bring food their way. Jellyfish have tentacles that can stretch for many metres, hanging below their bodies. Jellyfish can swim, or they are carried along by the sea's currents.

Mantis shrimps are mighty crustaceans. They punch or spear their prey, using such incredible force and speed that they are regarded as one of the most powerful animals in the world for their size. These small animals are common in Australian coral reefs and parts of the Indo-Pacific reef system.

▼ A blue-ringed octopus is only 20 centimetres long but its saliva contains poison that is strong enough to kill a human.

▲ Box jellyfish have such deadly stings that beaches are often closed in Australia when they are present in the water.

I DON'T BELIEVE IT!

Mantis shrimps are powerful punchers. They surprise their prey by hitting out at speeds of 240 metres per second.

Living together

The animals and plants that live on coral reefs need each other to survive. The close relationship between some animals is known as 'symbiosis'. Sometimes these partnerships give benefits to both animals, but at other times one animal gains little.

Coral polyps and their zooxanthellae are best buddies. Each zooxanthellae is made of just one cell. Like green plants, zooxanthellae make food using sunlight, water and carbon dioxide – a gas that is in the air. This process is called photosynthesis. The food they make is eaten by the polyps. Because they need sunlight to grow, zooxanthellae live inside a polyp's tentacles where light can reach them.

▼ Clownfish can hide among the stinging tentacles of a sea anemone without getting stung.

▲ Remora fish use other animals – such as this green turtle – to hitch a ride and find food.

I DON'T BELIEVE IT!

Boxer crabs use stinging sea anemones like boxing gloves. They wave them at any predators who get too close!

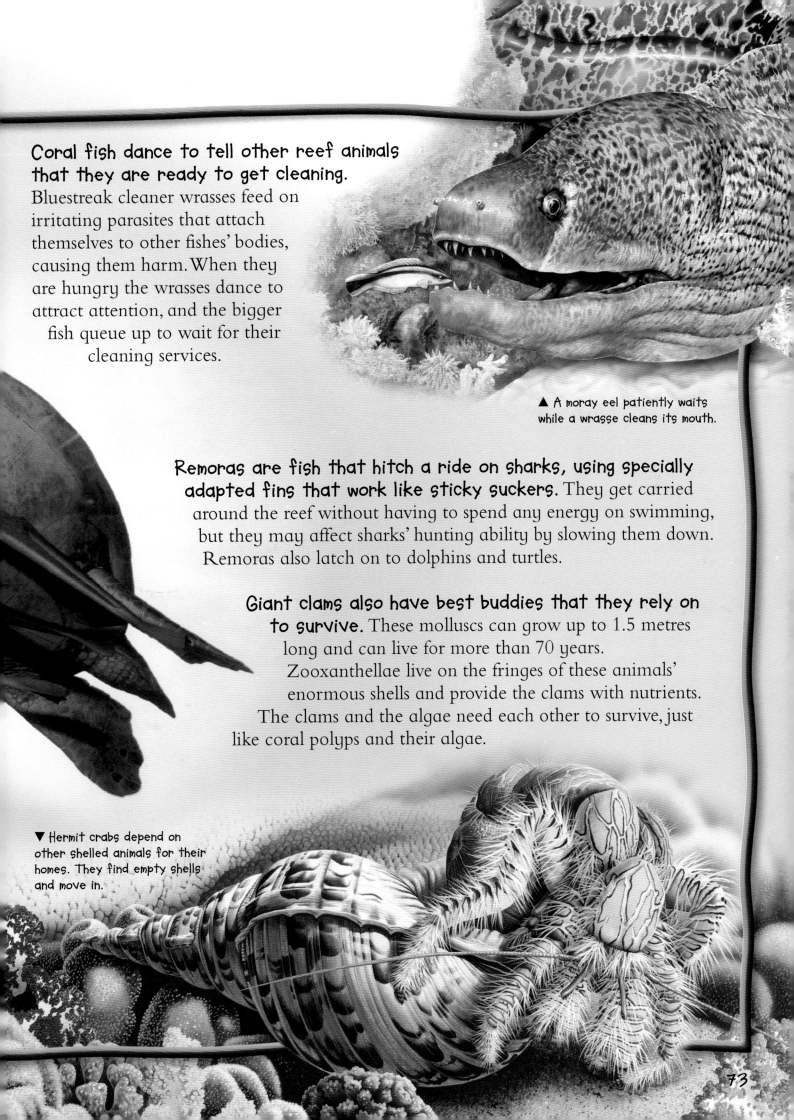

Coral fish dance to tell other reef animals that they are ready to get cleaning.
Bluestreak cleaner wrasses feed on irritating parasites that attach themselves to other fishes' bodies, causing them harm. When they are hungry the wrasses dance to attract attention, and the bigger fish queue up to wait for their cleaning services.

▲ A moray eel patiently waits while a wrasse cleans its mouth.

Remoras are fish that hitch a ride on sharks, using specially adapted fins that work like sticky suckers. They get carried around the reef without having to spend any energy on swimming, but they may affect sharks' hunting ability by slowing them down. Remoras also latch on to dolphins and turtles.

Giant clams also have best buddies that they rely on to survive. These molluscs can grow up to 1.5 metres long and can live for more than 70 years. Zooxanthellae live on the fringes of these animals' enormous shells and provide the clams with nutrients. The clams and the algae need each other to survive, just like coral polyps and their algae.

▼ Hermit crabs depend on other shelled animals for their homes. They find empty shells and move in.

Night on the reef

As the Sun sets over the ocean, coral reefs change. Polyps emerge from their cups and unfurl their tentacles, producing a range of colours and movements. Creatures that were active in daylight rest in dark crevices, while others emerge to feed in the dark.

Coral animals that come out at night are described as nocturnal. They often have senses that help them to detect movement, light, sound and chemicals in the inky-blue seas. Octopuses have superb night vision and long tentacles that they use to probe cracks in the reef, searching for food.

Coral reef spiny lobsters march through the night. At the end of the summer 100,000 of them set off on a long journey. Walking in single file towards deeper, darker water, they can travel up to 50 kilometres every night to reach their breeding grounds.

▼ A Christmas tree worm buries its body deep inside a coral. Only its two feeding tentacles, which look like trees, are visible.

◀ Corals are nocturnal and are most active at night.

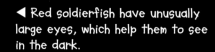

◄ Red soldierfish have unusually large eyes, which help them to see in the dark.

Divers can swim with giant stingrays at night. These enormous fish can measure up to 2 metres across and they often glide through the water in groups, gently flapping their 'wings' to move silently and swiftly. Stingrays do not need light to hunt because they are able to detect the electricity inside other animals' bodies, and use this information to find prey such as clams and oysters.

Fireworms are rarely seen in the day. They live under rocks and have venom-filled spines on their backs, giving them a furry appearance. During the summer adult worms emerge once at night, during a full moon, to mate. The females produce a green glow that attracts the males in the dark water.

▼ Mandarin fish rest during the day, but come out of their rocky shelters at night to hunt and feed.

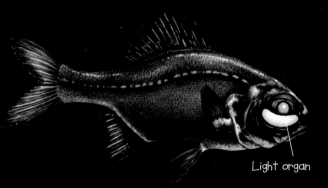

Light organ

▲ Most flashlight fish live in deep waters, where their ability to make light is most useful. Some types, however, swim into coral waters at night.

Relying on reefs

Millions of people rely on coral reefs for their survival. These ecosystems not only support fish and other animals, they also protect coastal regions from damage by storms and wave action.

▲ The people from this fishing village in Borneo depend on the reef for food.

There are around 500 types of seaweeds living on the Great Barrier Reef alone. Seaweeds contain substances that are useful to humans. Agar comes from red seaweeds and is used to make desserts, or to thicken soups and ice-cream. Alginates come from brown seaweeds and they are used to make cosmetics, thicken drinks and in the manufacture of paper and textiles.

Ecosystems that have a large range of living things are often used in medical science. Many species of animals and plants that live on reefs are being used in the search for new medicines that will cure illnesses. Substances in coral polyps are being used to develop treatments for some diseases, and to help rebuild broken bones.

▶ Collecting food, such as fish, and precious coral is a traditional way to survive in many places where reefs grow.

People who live around reefs have traded in coral products for thousands of years. The harvesting of red and pink corals for jewellery has caused many people to worry that the coral may be driven to extinction. Jewellery makers are asked to only use a small amount of coral every year and to only take coral from places where it will be protected as it regrows.

Coral reefs help to support local communities through tourism. Millions of people flock to the world's reefs to enjoy nature's underwater spectacle. The money they spend there helps support local people, who provide accommodation, food and equipment. Reefs are worth much more alive than dead. While one shark could be killed and sold for food, it is worth at least one hundred times more alive as an attraction to reef tourists.

▼ A trained guide shows tourists the delights of the Great Barrier Reef. 'Ecotourism' allows visitors to enjoy the reef without damaging it.

QUIZ

What am I?
1. I am used to thicken ice cream and soups.
2. I travel and visit places of interest.
3. I grow on the reef and am often made into jewellery.

Answers:
1. Agar 2. Tourist 3. Red and pink coral

Underwater explorers

Exploring a reef is a magical experience. Bathed in warm, blue water, a diver can swim among thousands of fish that dart around the coral. As schools of small, silvery fish flash past, smaller groups of predator fish follow – fast and alert in the chase.

CREATE A CORAL

Use quick-dry clay to create your own corals, copying the pictures in this book to get the right shapes. Once dry, paint the corals in bright colours. You can also make fish or other wildlife, to build your own coral reef ecosystem.

People have been fascinated by coral reefs for thousands of years. They have enjoyed watching reef wildlife, but they have also explored in search of food and building materials. Since coral reefs grow in shallow, clear water swimmers can enjoy them without any special equipment. Snorkels allow swimmers to breathe while their faces are in water.

The best way to explore a coral reef is to go underwater. Scuba equipment allows a diver to swim and breathe below the water's surface. Using an oxygen tank, flippers and a face mask a diver can move carefully around a reef, watching the creatures or carrying out scientific studies.

▼ Special equipment allows divers to photograph underwater wildlife such as this Goliath grouper.

Scientists have been examining coral reefs for more than 300 years. There are many research centres and universities near large coral reefs, so scientists can collect information and learn about the reefs over many years. There are even underwater research laboratories, where scientists can study reefs close up for days at a time.

▼ Divers explore old reefs, but they also visit places where new reefs are forming on shipwrecks, to understand how they develop.

Exploring reefs is fascinating, but it can be dangerous too. Curious blacktip reef sharks may give a diver a warning nip, but a sting from a box jellyfish can be deadly. There are also poisonous sea snakes, octopuses, shellfish and fish.

Natural coral Killers

Some fish not only live on a reef, they eat it too. There are more than 130 types of fish, known as corallivores, that feed on corals. They eat the slimy mucus made by polyps, the polyps themselves and even their stony cups. They like eating polyps during their breeding season because they are full of juicy, tasty eggs.

▲ Most coral-eating fish are butterfly fish. They have small mouths that can nibble at polyps and their eggs.

Reef-killing creatures have different eating habits around the world. In some regions, the coral-eating fish remove so much of the reef that it does not appear to grow at all. Threadfin butterfly fish in the Indian Ocean munch through large amounts of coral, but those that live around the Great Barrier Reef never eat coral. Corallivores that live in Caribbean reefs can survive on other food, too.

▼ Parrotfish change their appearance throughout their lives — they change colour as they grow up!

Parrotfish are dazzling in their appearance, but deadly in their lifestyle. They dig at coral with their tough mouths, which are like beaks, and grind it up in their throats. This releases the zooxanthellae that are an important part of their diet. The stony parts of the coral pass through their bodies, coming out the other end as beautiful white sand.

▲ Crown-of-thorns starfish graze on corals, especially in places where the starfish's natural enemy, the trumpet shellfish, has disappeared.

The crown-of-thorns starfish is one of the world's most famous coral-killers. It is covered in spines and can have as many as 21 'arms'. This starfish eats coral by turning its mouth inside out and pouring strong juices over the polyps to dissolve their flesh. It prefers fast-growing corals over the slower-growing types. The starfish eat the polyps, but leave the stony structure behind.

In the 1980s, Caribbean black sea urchins, called diademas, were wiped out by a deadly disease. These sea urchins kept the reefs healthy by grazing on seaweeds. Once they had died, seaweeds took over the coral, using up space and blocking out light. Seaweed-eating fish were also struggling to survive because too many of them had been caught by fishermen. There was nothing left to control the growth of seaweed and so the coral ecosystem was changed, and may never return to its previous, healthy state.

I DON'T BELIEVE IT!

Sponges are boring animals — they bore right into coral reefs! These simple animals dig right into the middle of a reef, making it weaker and more likely to collapse in storms.

Reefs at risk

Coral reefs are fragile ecosystems that are under threat from humans. When they are stressed, coral polyps lose their zooxanthellae, and die. Once the polyps have died the coral structure that is left appears white, and is described as 'bleached'.

▼ If zooxanthellae leave the coral, the polyps die. Over time, other types of algae and bacteria grow over the bleached coral.

1. Healthy coral with zooxanthellae living in coral tissue

2. Zooxanthellae leave coral due to increased water temperatures

3. Algae cover the damaged coral

▶ Global warming, a rise in worldwide temperatures, is caused by the polluting effects of carbon dioxide. It is raising sea temperatures and is causing coral bleaching.

Pollution, such as human waste (sewage) and chemicals used in farming, kills coral. In some places, pipes carry sewage to the sea where it mixes with the seawater. Sewage contains substances that feed seaweeds but bleach corals. On land, chemicals are used on crops to help them grow or to kill pests, but they get carried out to sea by rainwater and rivers, where they damage the reef and its inhabitants.

Tourists enjoy reefs, but they also put them at risk. Visitors put pressure on local ecosystems because they need food, transport and places to stay – which means pollution, fishing and building. Some tourists damage reefs by standing on them or touching them, and by buying wildlife souvenirs such as coral jewellery.

Damage to nearby land causes reefs to die. When coastal areas are changed by building or digging, soil is loosened and makes its way into the sea. Soil and dirt in seawater make it cloudy and stop sunlight from reaching the zooxanthellae. The result is more coral bleaching.

▶ Coral is broken up and taken from the sea to be used as a building material.

Catching and killing fish adds to the bleaching of coral reefs. In some parts of the world, fishermen use destructive methods of fishing. They drop bombs in the water, which explode and kill whole schools of fish, turning coral to crumbs. They also use chemicals, such as cyanide, to kill or stun fish.

SAVE OUR REEFS!
Make a poster to show the different ways coral reefs are being damaged and destroyed. Include a list of top tips for tourists to help them enjoy reefs safely without harming these ecosystems.

Conserving coral

Saving our coral reefs is incredibly important. We need to protect them, or it is likely they will become the first major ecosystem to become extinct in modern times. Setting up national parks, and stopping all forms of fishing means that reefs can develop naturally.

Artificial reefs have been built to replace the natural ones that are under threat. Some man-made reefs have been successful but scientists now agree that saving the coral reefs we have is the best option. They are working to find new ways to save coral polyps and help them recover once their natural environment has been damaged.

All parts of a coral reef ecosystem need to be protected. Removing one part, such as a single type of fish, can have terrible effects on other animals and plants that live there. Supporting local people as they find alternative ways to make money and find food, rather than relying on reefs is an important step forward.

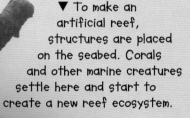

▼ To make an artificial reef, structures are placed on the seabed. Corals and other marine creatures settle here and start to create a new reef ecosystem.

The Komodo National Park in Indonesia covers 1817 square kilometres of land and sea. Tourists pay to support the workers and scientists who protect their natural environment, prevent illegal fishing and study the coral ecosystems in the park.

▲ Satellite photos of protected reefs, such as Hawaii's Pearl and Hermes atoll, help scientists find out how reefs are changing.

Scientists believe many coral reefs can be saved if they are protected now. Pollution is one of the biggest coral killers, and removing it could have an immediate effect on reefs' survival. This will give us more time to tackle the big problem of global warming, which will take many years.

▶ The ocean waters surrounding Komodo cover more than two-thirds of the National Park.

QUIZ

1. What do scientists believe could help save coral reefs?
2. Which word beginning with 'a' means man-made?
3. Why are national parks set up?

Answers:
1. Stopping pollution 2. Artificial 3. To protect endangered ecosystems

SEASHORE

Seashores can be found all over the world, from icy coastlines near the Poles to sandy beaches in hot, tropical areas. As well as making unique habitats (natural homes) for many plants and animals, seashores are also very important to people. Today, large areas of Earth's 700,000-plus kilometres of seashores are in danger and in need of our protection.

▼ Tall columns of rock (stacks), tidal pools, seaweeds and starfish are typical of rocky shores. This peaceful summer scene is at Second Beach near La Push, Washington State, USA.

Land meets sea

Seashores are places where the salty water of seas and oceans meets land made of rocks, mud, sand or other material. A seashore is the edge of the land and the edge of the sea.

Wave-shaped icebergs, Iceland

ARCTIC OCEAN

Tourist centre, Mexico

NORTH AMERICA

PACIFIC OCEAN

ATLANTIC OCEAN

There are names for different kinds of seashores. If the rocks are tall and upright, they are known as cliffs. If the sand is smooth and slopes gently, it is a beach. Seashores are known as oceanic coasts, or marine or sea coastlines.

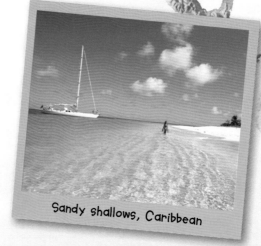
Sandy shallows, Caribbean

SOUTH AMERICA

Water moves easily with waves, tides and currents, so seashores are never still. They are complicated habitats for nature, as only certain kinds of animals and plants can live there. Wildlife must be able to survive in the changing conditions that are typical of most seashores.

Breaking glaciers, Antarctica

SOUTHERN OCEAN

Seafront houses, Denmark

EUROPE

ASIA

PACIFIC OCEAN

AFRICA

Great Barrier Reef, Australia

Tropical palm beach, Seychelles

OCEANIA

INDIAN OCEAN

In total, there are more than 700,000 kilometres of seashore. Canada is the country with the longest total seashore, at more than 202,000 kilometres. Indonesia is next, with 55,000 kilometres of seashore.

Some seashores are not part of the world's main network of seas and oceans. They are the seashores around the edges of large bodies of salty water that are isolated inland, such as the Caspian Sea and the Dead Sea.

ANTARCTICA

Endless battles

Seashores are like battlegrounds, with a continuing struggle between land and sea. The outcome depends on factors such as the land's hardness, and the strength of the winds and waves.

Waves

Cliff

Cliff undercut by crashing waves

Rocks from fallen cliff

Sand

Pebbles

▶ Winds provide the energy to whip up waves that erode the shore.

The sea's power is immense. Winds, waves, tides and currents wear away (erode) the land. Big waves hit the shore with enough energy to throw around boulders the size of cars. Even small waves roll around tiny bits of rock that rub and scour the land.

In some places the sea wins the battle along the shore. The land is gradually rubbed away, or parts collapse and slide into the water. The pieces, or particles, are swept away by waves, tides and currents.

▼ In East Anglia, England, soft coastal rocks are worn away by up to 5 metres each year. Houses that were once inland end up as rubble underwater.

▲ These granite rocks in Nova Scotia, Canada, have hardly changed for hundreds of years.

▲ Chalk cliffs in southern England are eaten away by waves, leaving piles of broken pieces at their bases.

How the seashore's land resists the eroding power of the sea depends on the types of rocks. Hard rocks, such as granite, are tough and can resist erosion for centuries. Softer rocks, such as chalk and mudstone, erode several metres each year.

In other places, the land wins the battle. New land can be formed from piles of particles, such as sand or silt, moved by the water from coasts elsewhere or from the deep sea. Particles sink and settle as layers, called sediments, that build up.

CLIFF COLLAPSE!

You will need:
large, deep tray or bowl
wet play sand   water

Make a steep cliff in the tray or bowl by piling up wetted sand on one side. Then gently pour in the water. Swish the water with your hand to make waves. Watch how they eat into the cliff and make it fall down.

Movements in the Earth can change seashores. Land can bend and buckle over centuries, so coasts slowly rise. Earthquakes can lift land by several metres in a few seconds. A volcano near the coast can spill its red-hot lava into the sea, where it cools as hard, new rock.

▶ Lava meets the sea in Hawaii. Sea water makes volcanic lava cool suddenly in a cloud of steam.

Tides, currents and winds

Almost all seashores have tides, which affect the way the land is worn away. Tides alter the amount of time that a particular patch of the shore is underwater or exposed to the air, so they also affect coastal habitats and wildlife.

Tides are caused by the pulling power or gravity of the Moon and Sun, and the daily spinning of the Earth. A high tide occurs about 12.5 hours after the previous high tide, with low tides midway between.

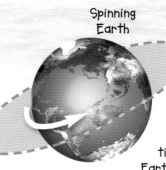

Moon

Spinning Earth

Tidal bulge

◄ The Moon's gravity pulls the sea into 'bulges' on the near and opposite sides, where it is high tide. Inbetween is low tide. As the Earth spins daily, the 'bulge' travels around the planet.

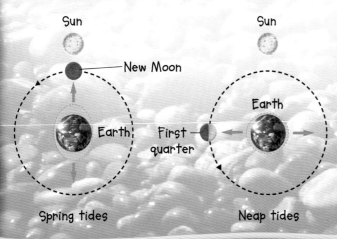

Spring tides are extra-high — the water level rises more than normal. They happen when the Moon and Sun are in line with the Earth, adding their gravities together every 14 days (two weeks). Neap tides are extra-low, when the Sun and Moon are at right angles, so their pulling strengths partly cancel each other out. A neap tide occurs seven days after a spring tide.

▼ At new Moon and full Moon, the Sun, Moon and Earth are in a straight line, causing spring tides. At the first and last quarters of the Moon, the Sun and Moon are not aligned, so neap tides occur.

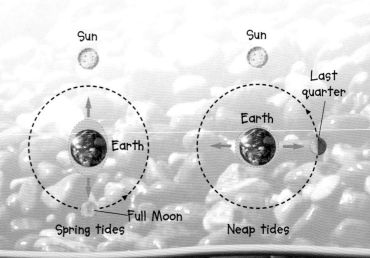

| Sun | Sun | Sun | Sun |

New Moon

First quarter

Full Moon

Last quarter

Earth

Earth

Earth

Earth

Spring tides — Neap tides — Spring tides — Neap tides

(4) Splash zone has lichens, which receive wave spray

(3) Upper intertidal zone is exposed to air most of the time – there are green wrack seaweeds and limpets

(2) Mid intertidal zone is submerged half of the time – there are mussels, barnacles, hermit crabs and brown seaweeds

(1) Lower intertidal zone is usually underwater – there are anemones, starfish, fish and red seaweeds

Tides produce 'zones' along seashores, from the high tide zone to the low tide zone. Different seaweeds and animals are adapted to each zone.

▲ The amount of time underwater determines which animals and plants live along a rocky shore.

Ocean currents affect the seashore. A current flowing towards the shore can bring particles of sediment to add to the land. A current flowing away sweeps sediment out to sea. Currents also alter the direction and power of waves.

If a wind blows waves at an angle onto a beach, each wave carries particles of sand upwards and sideways. When they recede, the particles roll back. Particles gradually zigzag along the shore – a process called longshore drift. Groynes built into the sea help to control it, so beaches don't wash away.

Seashore features

On a typical seashore, the struggle between land and sea produces various features. Much depends on the balance between the sea's wearing away of the land, and the formation of new land by particles settling in layers, known as sedimentation.

Stack

Headlan

Arch

Stump

Needle

Shingle spit

Shingle or pebble beach

Groyne

Hard or tough rocks can resist the sea's eroding power. They form tall cliffs and headlands that erode slowly. Softer rocks break apart more easily. The waves erode them at sea level, which is known as undercutting. The whole shore collapses as boulders tumble into the water.

Waves and other shore-eroding forces may gradually cut through a headland, forming a cave. This can get worn through to form an arch of rock. When the arch collapses it leaves an isolated tall piece of rock, called a stack.

▲ In this bay, waves and currents wash sediments with increasing power from right to left. Wall-like groynes or breakwaters lessen longshore drift.

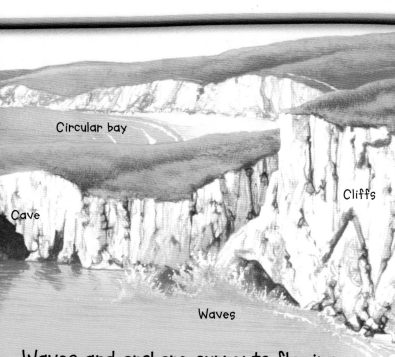

Circular bay

Cave

Cliffs

Waves

Waves and onshore currents flowing towards the land bring sediments to make low shores and mounds of sand, mud and silt. These can lengthen to form long spits. During extra-high spring tides these sediments grow higher.

Depending on winds and currents, a huge rounded scoop may be carved along the seashore to form a bay. In sheltered parts of the bay, particles of sand gather to form a beach. As the bay gets more curved, it can break through the land behind to leave an island.

River →

Delta

Mudflats (bare mud near delta)

Saltmarsh (with plants)

Sandy beach

The area where a river flows into the sea is a type of shore known as an estuary, or river mouth. Particles of sand and mud may build up in sheltered areas, forming low mudflats and saltmarshes.

Coast to coast

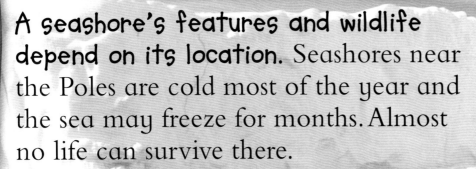

A seashore's features and wildlife depend on its location. Seashores near the Poles are cold most of the year and the sea may freeze for months. Almost no life can survive there.

◄ Antarctic coasts are mostly floating sheets and lumps of ice. Crabeater seals rest at the ice edge after feeding in the almost freezing water.

Some cold seashores have no land. Glaciers and ice shelves spread outwards, so the sea meets ice, not land. The edge of the ice may have smooth slopes and platforms cut by the waves. Jagged chunks of ice crack off and fall into the water as floating icebergs.

In tropical regions around the middle of the Earth, seashore conditions are very different. It is warm for most of the year and many forms of life flourish, including seaweeds, fish, crabs, prawns, starfish and corals.

▼ Tropical seashores include coral reefs, like this one near Komodo Island, Southeast Asia, with huge biodiversity (range of living things).

Exposure to wind is a powerful factor in the shaping of a shoreline. A windward seashore is exposed to strong prevailing winds. The winds make waves that hit the shore hard, sending salty spray to great heights. This type of shore has very different animals and plants from a leeward seashore, which is sheltered from the main winds.

Yearly seasons have an effect on seashores and their wildlife. Usually there is rough weather in winter, with winds and storms that increase land erosion. Some wildlife moves away from the shore in winter – birds fly inland while lobsters and fish move into deeper water.

The slope of the sea bed at the shore is very important, affecting the size and number of waves. A sea bed with a very shallow slope tends to produce smaller waves. A steep slope up to the beach gives bigger waves that erode the land faster, but are good for surfing!

LET'S SURF!

You will need:
sink or bathtub   water   tray

Put 10 centimetres of water into the sink or bathtub. Hold the tray at one end, at an angle so that part of it slopes into the water like a beach. Swish your other hand in the water to make waves hit the 'beach'. How does altering the tray's angle from low to high affect the waves?

▲ A big winter storm, such as this one in Sussex, UK, can smash even the strongest sea defences, which have to be repaired regularly.

Saltmarshes and mudflats

Sea thrift (sea pink) likes drier areas of marsh

Common cordgrass helps bind loose mud

Glasswort has fleshy leaves that store water

Sea aster flowers in late summer

▲ Saltmarsh plants have to endure harsh conditions, as they are exposed to both salt water and freshwater.

On a sheltered seashore, small particles of sediment collect. This happens around the mouths of rivers (estuaries). As the river's water speed slows, its floating particles sink to the bottom.

Saltmarshes have partly dry areas. They are rarely fully submerged, perhaps only with salty water at spring tides, or with freshwater if a nearby river floods.

▶ Many wading birds feed by probing into mud for small worms and shellfish.

Redshank

Curlew

Saltmarsh plants include glasswort, sea purslane, sea aster, sea lavender, sea thrift and red fescue. These plants are food for small creatures such as worms and insects, which are eaten by birds such as rails, curlews, herons and egrets.

Mudflats are usually lower and wetter than saltmarshes, as every high tide washes over them. Plants find it difficult to take root in these conditions, but a few, such as rice grass, cordgrass and eel grass, manage. Cordgrass grows in the wetter regions of saltmarshes around the world. It has glands to get rid of unwanted salt taken in from sea water.

Soft-shell clams like muddy shores best

Laver spireshells are also called mudsnails

Towershells feed in both sand and silt

Common cockles filter sea water for food

Most mudflat animal life is under the surface. There are burrowing animals such as ragworms, mud shrimps and ghost crabs, and shelled creatures such as spireshells, towershells, cockles and various types of clams. Birds, especially waders such as godwits, knots and snipes, fly in at low tide to probe for these creatures.

▼ Each year, summer plants grow into the calm waters of saltmarshes, spreading their greenery into the channels. However autumn storms soon wash them away.

▲ Shelled animals with two shell halves are called bivalves. Spiral ones are types of sea-snails.

I DON'T BELIEVE IT!
In some mudflats, the numbers of small shellfish, called spireshells, are greater than 50,000 in just one square metre!

Sandy beaches

Sandy shores need gentle winds, waves and currents that are still strong enough to wash away silt and mud. Just above high tide, any rain quickly drains away between the grains of sand, so it is too dry for land plants to grow. Below this, the grains move with wind, waves and tides, so few sea plants can grow there either.

Most sandy shore life is under the surface. Animals hide under the sand while the tide is out. As it rises, it brings with it tiny plants and animals, known as plankton, and bits of dead plants and creatures. Shrimps, lugworms, clams, tellins, scallops and heart urchins burrow through the sand or filter the water to feed.

Small sandy shore animals are meals for bigger predators that follow the tide, including cuttlefish, octopus and fish such as sea bass and flatfish. The giant sea bass of North Pacific shores grows to more than 2 metres long and weighs 250 kilograms.

Jellyfish
may get washed up onto the beach and stranded

Cuttlefish
grab prey with their tentacles

▼ As the tide comes in, creatures hidden in the sand come out and start to feed — but predators are ready to eat them.

Sand eels
feed on the bottom

Flatfish
have colours similar to the sea bed

Common shrimps
half-hide in burrows

▼ Fencing helps to keep sand dunes still, so grasses can start to grow.

As high tide retreats, it leaves a ribbon of washed-up debris along a beach, called the strandline. Animals including gulls, foxes, otters and lizards scavenge here for food, such as dead fish and crabs.

On some sandy shores, onshore winds blow the sand grains up the beach towards the land. Mounds, ridges and hills form seashore habitats called sand dunes. Marram grass can survive the wind and dryness, and its roots stop the grains blowing away, stabilizing the dunes.

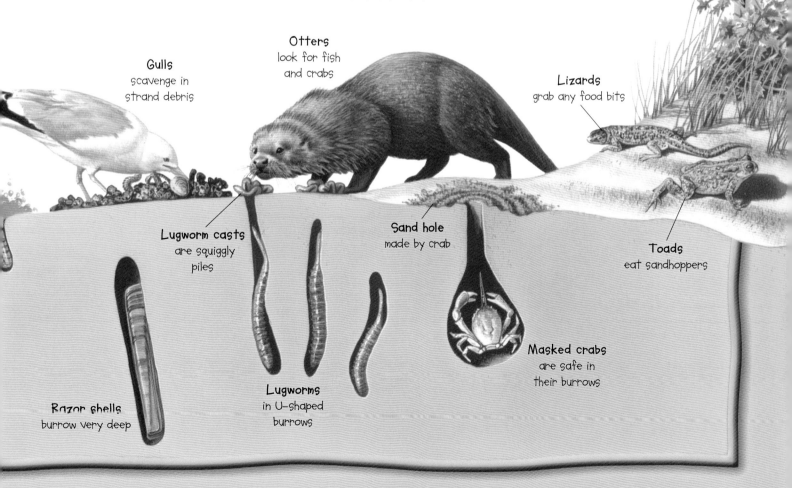

Gulls
scavenge in strand debris

Otters
look for fish and crabs

Lizards
grab any food bits

Lugworm casts
are squiggly piles

Sand hole
made by crab

Toads
eat sandhoppers

Razor shells
burrow very deep

Lugworms
in U-shaped burrows

Masked crabs
are safe in their burrows

Mangrove swamps

Mangrove swamps are unusual shore habitats. They occur in the tropics where wind, waves and currents are weak, allowing mud to collect. The mud has no tiny air pockets, which land plants need to take oxygen from.

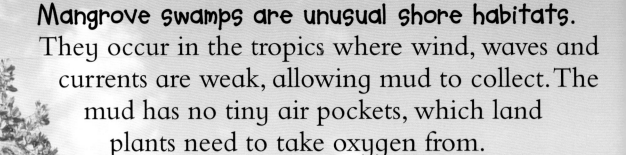

◀ Shoreline mangroves, here in East Africa, form a thick tangle where no other plants grow. These mangrove trees have stilt roots.

Mangrove trees use their unusual roots to get oxygen from the air. Some have stilt or prop roots, which hold the tree above the mud and water so it can take in oxygen through tiny holes in its bark. Others have aerial roots covered with tiny holes that poke above the mud into the air.

▼ Black mangroves, like these in Florida, USA, have aerial roots covered with tiny holes that poke above the mud into the air.

Mangrove swamps teem with wildlife. The biggest creatures include dugongs and manatees (large marine mammals) that eat the fallen leaves, flowers and fruits of mangrove trees. Fish and turtles swim among the roots, while mangrove and fiddler crabs burrow in the mud or climb the roots.

▲ Mangrove roots, stems and seaweeds form an underwater jungle where small predators, such as this lemon shark pup, hunt for victims.

Roosting birds, land crabs, mangrove snakes and fishing cats live in mangroves. In South and Southeast Asia, tigers slink between the trees looking for prey. One of the strangest inhabitants is the proboscis monkey. The male has a long, floppy nose, which can be up to 8 centimetres in length.

Male proboscis monkey

Female proboscis monkey

▶ Proboscis monkeys eat mainly mangrove leaves and fruits, and they are excellent swimmers.

Baby proboscis monkey

QUIZ

Match these mangrove creatures with their food.
1. White-bellied mangrove snake 2. Tiger 3. Proboscis monkey
A. Mangrove leaves, buds, flowers and fruits
B. Large prey, such as monkeys and deer
C. Small crabs and fish

Answers:
1C 2B 3A

Shingle and pebbles

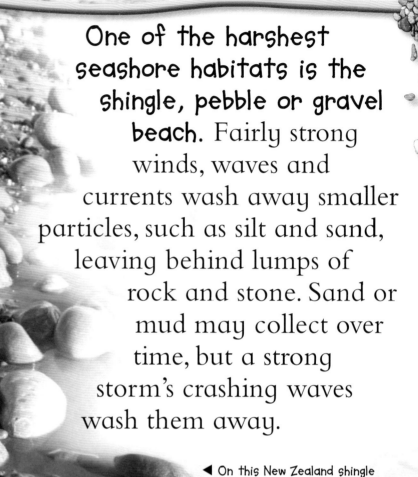

One of the harshest seashore habitats is the shingle, pebble or gravel beach. Fairly strong winds, waves and currents wash away smaller particles, such as silt and sand, leaving behind lumps of rock and stone. Sand or mud may collect over time, but a strong storm's crashing waves wash them away.

◀ On this New Zealand shingle beach, a storm has washed away some of the smaller pebbles to leave a line of larger cobbles, which protect the shingle higher up.

HIDDEN EGGS

You will need:
smooth, rounded pebbles   tray
watercolour paints and brush
three hen's eggs

Lay out the pebbles on the tray and look at their colours and patterns. Paint the hen's eggs to match the pebbles. Place the eggs among the pebbles. Are they so well camouflaged that your friends can't spot them?

Waves roll shingle and pebbles around, wearing away their sharp edges and making them smooth and rounded. Plants are in danger of being crushed by the waves, but oysterplant, sea kale and sea blite gain a roothold. Lichens, combinations of fungi or moulds, and simple plants known as algae, coat the stones.

◀ Sea kale usually grows just above the high tide mark.

Ring-like black band around neck

Camouflaged eggs

Fleshy folded leaves

Plentiful small white flowers

Animals forage along the strandline, where debris is left by the receding high tide. Ringed plovers, little terns and oystercatchers lay their eggs in a small scrape or hollow. The eggs are perfectly camouflaged because they look similar to the pebbles around them.

▲ The ringed plover checks its eggs before going off to feed on small creatures.

Shingle and pebble shores are very mobile. Storms and powerful currents can shift them from place to place, or even wash them into the sea. Pebbles can build up over years into a long ridge called a shingle spit. The spit shelters the sea behind it and allows other kinds of coastlines to form, such as mudflats, lagoons or sandy beaches.

◀ The 16-kilometre shingle spit of Orford Ness, east England, is bare on the seaward side, but has plants on the sheltered side bordering the River Alde.

Estuaries and lagoons

▲ This maze of channels and sandbanks at the mouth of Australia's Murray River changes over months and years, especially during winter storms.

An estuary is the end of a river at the coast, where it flows into the sea. The river might emerge through a narrow gap. Or it can gradually widen as it approaches the sea, so that at the shore it is so wide you cannot see from one side to the other.

The river water slows down as it flows into the sea and loses its movement energy. As this happens, its sediment particles settle out in order of size. This is known as sediment sorting or grading. As particles settle to the bottom, they may form a spreading area in the river mouth called a delta.

Estuaries are halfway habitats, with freshwater towards the river and salt water towards the sea. There is an ever-changing mixture inbetween due to tides, currents and rainfall. This partly salty water is known as brackish.

▶ Grizzly bears dig up tasty shellfish on an estuary beach in Canada.

► This circular island in the Maldives, called a coral atoll, has a lagoon in the middle.

A lagoon is a sheltered area behind some kind of barrier, such as a ridge of shingle or a coral reef. Protected from the full force of the waves, lagoons are usually calm, warm, shallow and full of life.

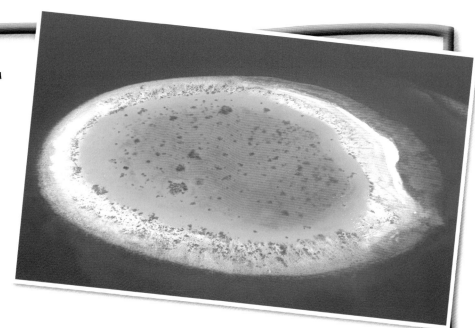

▼ Blacktip reef sharks often gather in shallow lagoons and estuaries in the breeding season to find partners and mate. They lay eggs here, where the baby sharks are safer from large predators than in the open water.

The tallest inhabitants in some coastal lagoons are flamingos, such as the American and greater flamingo. They filter tiny shrimps, shellfish and plants from the water with the brush-like bristles inside their beaks.

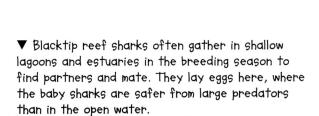

Rocky shores and pools

Where the land is made from hard rock, different kinds of rocky shores form. They vary with the rock's hardness, the size of the pieces, and whether the shore is exposed to wind, waves and currents. Tidal zones (see page 93) are usually visible on these shores with 'lines' of seaweeds.

▲ Some seaweeds, such as kelps, have a sucker-like part, the holdfast, to fix them to rocks.

▼ Seaweeds anchor to any stable object, such as these mostly buried rocks on a beach in France.

Channelled wrack, a green seaweed, often grows high on the shore with bladderwrack. Knotted rack grows slightly lower. Towards the low tide area are brown seaweeds, such as oarweeds and kelps, and even lower are red seaweeds. These plants vary depending on the coast's exposure to wind and waves.

KEY

1. Anemone
2. Mussel
3. Goby
4. Bladderwrack seaweed
5. Hermit crab
6. Topshell
7. Limpet
8. Razor shell
9. Sea urchin
10. Sponge
11. Shore crab
12. Velvet crab
13. Prawn
14. Starfish

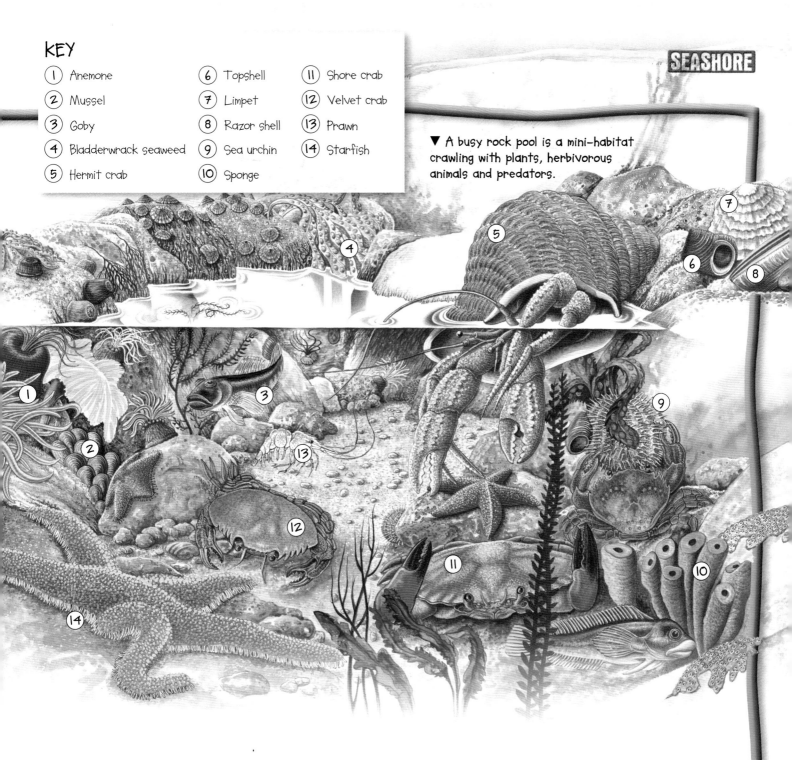

▼ A busy rock pool is a mini-habitat crawling with plants, herbivorous animals and predators.

Fixed-down creatures such as barnacles and mussels live on the bare rocks of the mid-tidal zones. As the tide comes in they filter tiny edible particles from the water. Limpets hold onto the rocks firmly and move slowly, scraping off plant growth. Seaweeds form forests for smaller animals such as shellfish, crabs, prawns, and fish such as gobies and blennies, as well as starfish, anemones, sea mats and sea squirts.

Seashore rock pools are left behind as the tide retreats. They are miniature communities of animals and plants. The seaweeds capture the Sun's light energy for growth. Herbivorous animals such as periwinkles and limpets eat the plants. Predators ranging from whelks to octopus hide among the crevices and prey on the herbivores.

Visitors to the shore

Many animals visit seashores. Some of them come to feed or breed. Others stop there to rest during long journeys or to escape danger such as predators or harsh conditions inland or out at sea. Otters like to catch fish and crabs in the pools and shallows.

▲ Sea lion pups may feed on their mother's milk for up to one year.

◀ Male Southern elephant seals roar and fight rivals on the beach. Winners get to mate with females.

Seals, sea lions and walruses are ideally suited to diving, swimming and feeding at sea. But they come ashore to beaches or rocks to rest and sunbathe.

Seals and sea lions have their young (pups) along the seashore. The pups feed on their mothers' milk, then stay ashore while the mothers return to the sea to catch food. Within two or three weeks the pups can swim and dive.

▲ Terns flock down to rest overnight on a remote beach before continuing their migration.

Visiting birds use seashores as resting places on their long yearly journeys (migrations). Some move to the coast for winter, when inland waters freeze. Migrants include waders or shorebirds such as dunlins, sandpipers, godwits and curlews. Wildfowl such as ducks, geese and swans also stop over on migration or overwinter on the shore.

Among the rarest shore visitors is the sea turtle. The female hauls herself up the beach under cover of darkness, scoops a large hole with her flippers, lays her eggs in it, covers them and lumbers back to the sea. Weeks later the baby turtles hatch and dig their way to the surface. Then it's a race to the sea – many will be eaten by gathering predators on the way.

▶ After laying about 150 eggs into the hole she dug, this female green turtle pushes sand on top to close the hole before returning to the water.

Above the seashore

The skies above many seashores are busy with all kinds of flying animals. Several kinds of birds rest or nest along the shore, flying out to sea or inland to feed.

◀ Different kinds of birds tend to perch and nest at different heights along the cliffs.

Coastal cliffs are safe nesting places for many different seabirds. It is difficult for predators, such as foxes, lizards or snakes, to reach the birds' eggs and chicks on steep rocky ledges. Cliff-nesters include fulmars, puffins, Manx shearwaters and gannets.

KEY

1. Great black-backed gull
2. Lesser black-backed gull
3. Herring gull
4. Rock dove
5. Chough
6. Puffin
7. Guillemot
8. Razorbill
9. Rock pipit
10. Fulmar
11. Kittiwake
12. Black guillemot

As darkness falls along the shore, most birds settle to rest. The nocturnal (night-time) fliers such as owls and bats come out. The coastal sheath-tail bat of Australia and Papua New Guinea feeds mainly on beetles and other insects. Along the shores of southwest North America, the fishing bat swoops down to catch fish, crabs and other creatures.

▲ The caracara, a type of falcon, pecks the flesh from mussels.

Some birds fly along coasts when looking for food, including gulls, waders, wildfowl and birds of prey. There are several types of sea eagle, including the bald eagle (national emblem of the USA) and the even more powerful Steller's sea eagle.

Flying insects are also common along seashores, especially in the summer. Beetles and flies buzz around washed-up rotting seaweeds, fish and other debris. Butterflies flutter along the upper shore and cliffs, searching for sweet nectar in the flowers. They include the bitterbush blue butterfly of Australia, and North America's rare Lange's metalmark butterfly, which inhabits sand dunes.

▶ Grayling butterflies sunbathe on sea holly and shore rocks.

Sea holly

I DON'T BELIEVE IT!

The peregrine falcon hunts along the shore as well as inland. It kills other birds by power-diving onto them at speeds of more than 200 kilometres an hour, making it the world's fastest animal.

Skins, shells and stars

Many kinds of small seashore fish, such as gobies, shannies and blennies, don't have scales. They are covered in tough, smooth, slippery skin. This helps them to wriggle through seaweed and slip away from rolling pebbles.

▲ The soft-bodied hermit crab uses an empty sea-snail shell for protection, finding a larger one as it grows.

▼ Mudskippers can stay out of water for several hours and 'skip' on their front fins.

Crabs scuttle and swim across the shore. They have eight walking legs and two strong pincers (chelae). Many are scavengers, eating whatever they can find. Others hunt small fish and similar creatures. Their long-bodied cousins are lobsters, which grow to one metre long.

FISHY FACTS!

You will need:
notebook   pen

Next time you're in a supermarket or fishmonger, look for the various kinds of fish and shellfish on sale – cod, salmon, prawns, mussels and so on. Make a list of them. Do some research and find out which ones live along seashores – probably quite a few!

Seashore anemones look like jelly blobs when the tide is out and colourful flowers when it's in. Anemones are predatory animals. Their stinging tentacles grab fish, shrimps and other prey, paralyze them, and pass them to the mouth.

Starfish are slow but deadly hunters. They grab shellfish such as mussels, and gradually pull their shell halves apart. The starfish then turns its stomach inside out through its mouth, and pushes this through the gap between the shell halves to digest the flesh within.

▼ The scallop snaps its two shell valves shut, creating a jet of water that pushes it away from danger, such as a hungry starfish.

Shellfish abound on the seashore. Whelks and topshells have snail-like curly shells. Cowries have beautifully patterned shells in bright colours. Bivalve shellfish such as clams, oysters, cockles and scallops have two halves (valves) to the shell.

▶ Goose barnacles are related to crabs. Their feathery feeding tentacles filter tiny bits of food from sea water.

Seashore dangers

Seashores can be hit by many types of natural disasters. Among the most deadly are giant waves called tsunamis. These are usually set off by underwater earthquakes, volcanoes or landslides, which shake the sea bed and push water into massive ripples that spread out until they reach a shore.

③ Wave gets taller but slower as it approaches the coast

② An upward wave is formed

④ Wave crashes or breaks onto the coast

① Undersea earthquake moves large amount of water

▲ As tsunami waves enter shallow water, they move more slowly but grow taller.

The high winds of hurricanes, typhoons and tornadoes can whip up giant waves. They crash on the shore, smash buildings, flood far inland and cause immense destruction. In 2008, typhoon Nargis hit Burma (Myanmar) in Southeast Asia. It killed more than 200,000 people, made millions homeless, and flooded vast areas with salt water, making the land useless for growing crops.

▼ Tsunamis can flood whole towns along the coast, washing salt water and mud everywhere. Houses were flattened near the coast of Banda Aceh, Indonesia, after a tsunami in 2004.

▲ In the past being a lighthouse-keeper was a vital but lonely job, with weeks alone tending the lamp and its machinery. Today most lighthouses, such as Fanad Head in north-west Ireland, are electric and mostly automatic.

For centuries fire beacons, lanterns, lighthouses and lightships have warned boats and ships about dangerous shores. Hazards include running aground on a sandbank or hitting rocks just under the surface. Each lighthouse flashes at a different time interval so sailors can identify it.

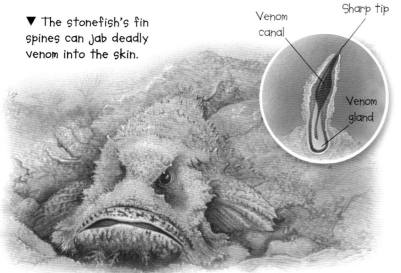

▼ The stonefish's fin spines can jab deadly venom into the skin.

Venom canal

Sharp tip

Venom gland

▼ Fire coral is named after the burning pain it causes if touched.

Even just walking along a shore or paddling in shallow water can be dangerous, especially in tropical regions. There may be poisonous animals such as jellyfish, weeverfish, stonefish and shellfish known as coneshells, all of which have stings that can kill.

People and seashores

People have lived along seashores and coastlines for thousands of years. Settlers could hunt and gather food from the sea. They could travel by boat along the coast, up rivers to inland areas and across the sea to other regions. These boats carried raw materials, food and goods for trading.

Foods from the seashore include fish, octopus, crabs and lobsters caught with nets, spears or hooks and lines. Shellfish such as cockles, mussels, scallops, limpets and winkles are gathered by hand. Seaweeds can be harvested for food or to obtain chemicals used in many processes from dyeing textiles to glass-making.

Seashores are important in traditional arts, crafts and religions. Driftwood is carved into fantastic shapes, seashells are collected for their beauty, and necklaces made of sharks' teeth supposedly give strength to the wearer. Gods and spirits from the sea feature in many religions, faiths and customs, such as Kauhuhu the shark god of Hawaii.

▼ Sri Lankan fishermen perch on poles and watch for fish passing below as the tide changes.

▲ Lights never go out in Hong Kong harbour, one of the world's busiest seaports.

▼ More than 150,000 troops landed on Normandy beaches in France on D-Day, 6 June, 1944.

In recent times, large areas of coastal land in places such as the Netherlands, India, Bangladesh and southern USA have been made into rich farmlands. Sea walls and other defences keep the waves at bay. Reclaimed land is used for factories and industry, dwellings (as in Venice and Singapore), and airport runways (as in Sydney, Singapore and Hong Kong).

▼ Holiday developments completely destroy natural coasts, with increased travel by air and sea as tourists come and go.

Seashores have featured in empires and battles through the ages. Seafaring and trading centres, such as Constantinople (now Istanbul), Venice and London, were once hubs of great empires. Castles and forts keep out seaborne invaders. World War II's D-Day seaborne invasion of France's Normandy coastline in 1944 was the largest military event in history.

Seaside adventures

In modern times, seashores have become places for fun, leisure and adventure. People relax, sunbathe, play games and sports, and view buildings and monuments. In many countries, more than half of all tourism business is along coasts.

▲ Scuba-divers should 'take nothing but photographs and memories', leaving wildlife completely untouched.

▼ Adding just the right amount of water makes the sand firm for sculpting.

Fun activities at the seashore include swimming, snorkelling, scuba-diving, kite-flying and building sandcastles. People also paint, draw and photograph beautiful scenes of the waves, shore, sky and Sun. Many seaside resorts have sand sculpture competitions, where contestants produce amazing shapes from just sand and water.

Some seashores attract sportspeople, especially large flat beaches, which can be used by horse riders, runners and racers. Sand racing takes many forms, from land-yachts with wheels blown along by sails, to record-breaking racing cars. Softer sand is best for volleyball, football, bowls and similar ball games.

SAND SCULPTING

You will need:
half a bucket of clean play sand
large tray   small cup   water

Start with dry sand. Pour it onto the tray and try to shape it into a tower or castle. Put it back in the bucket, mix in one cup of water and try again. Then add another cup, try again, and so on. At what stage is the sand best for shaping and sculpting?

In shallow water along the shore, people do sports such as surfing, windsurfing, kitesurfing, waterskiing, jetskiing and paragliding. There is also rod fishing, spear fishing, beach netting and other pastimes which could result in a tasty meal.

Sea walls and pleasure piers extend from the shore, allowing people to stroll along, do some sea fishing or see a show in the theatre at the end. The longest pleasure pier in the world is Southend Pier in Essex, England, at 2160 metres.

▼ Bondi Beach near Sydney, Australia, is famous for its surfing and lifesaving displays — but it also gets very crowded.

▼ Pleasure piers, such as Southend Pier, were popular in the last century, but few new ones are built.

Trade and power

▶ Modern ports, such as this one in Singapore, are busy day and night all through the year.

Cities, ports and industrial centres have been set up along seashores all over the world. There are harbours, docks, wharves and warehouses where cargo ships and passengers come and go, as part of global trade and travel.

Today's world uses energy at an increasing rate and many energy sources come through or from seashores. Petroleum (oil) and gas supertankers arrive at coastal storage centres, depots and refineries, where they load or unload their cargoes.

Many electricity-generating power stations are along seashores. Big ships can unload supplies of coal, oil, gas and other energy sources directly to them. Another reason is that they can use sea water to cool their generating equipment, to make electricity more efficiently.

▲ At Mossel Bay, South Africa, dozens of giant tanks store natural gas from wells out at sea.

Electricity can be generated at seashores, especially from the moving water of tides and waves. The flowing water turns underwater turbine blades connected to generators when the tide comes in and goes out. Wave power is more difficult to harness because big storms can smash the generating equipment.

Factories making products are often sited along the coast. Cargo ships bring raw materials, such as coal, oil and metal ores, and take away finished products ranging from MP3 players to giant trucks. Unfortunately, factory wastes and unwanted chemicals may flow or discharge along pipes into the sea.

▲ The Limpet is one type of small wave-power generator being tested in Scotland.

Seashores in trouble

Seashores and their animals and plants face all sorts of threats and dangers. Pollution occurs in many forms, such as oil spills, chemical waste from factories, and dirty water and sewage from towns and cities. All kinds of rubbish litters the shore.

▲ In Namibia, Africa, desert comes right to the sea. Many ships have run aground and been wrecked, rusting away along this 'Skeleton Coast'.

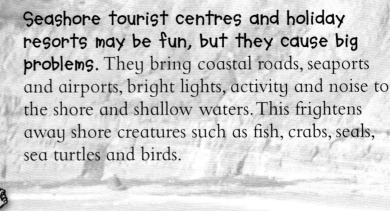

Seashore tourist centres and holiday resorts may be fun, but they cause big problems. They bring coastal roads, seaports and airports, bright lights, activity and noise to the shore and shallow waters. This frightens away shore creatures such as fish, crabs, seals, sea turtles and birds.

▼ This pile of plastic and other debris in Dorset, England, is typical of the pollution washed up after a storm.

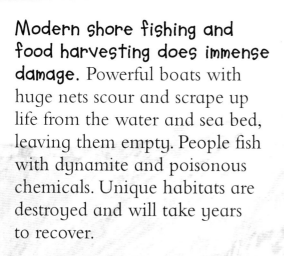

Modern shore fishing and food harvesting does immense damage. Powerful boats with huge nets scour and scrape up life from the water and sea bed, leaving them empty. People fish with dynamite and poisonous chemicals. Unique habitats are destroyed and will take years to recover.

▲ Plastic nets and lines do not rot away naturally. They may trap animals, such as this green turtle, for months.

Global warming and climate change are looming problems for the whole Earth – especially seashores. Sea levels will rise, altering the shapes of coasts, wiping out natural shore habitats and man-made ones, and flooding low-lying land beyond, from wild areas to cities and rich farmland.

With global warming and climate change, more extreme weather may come along coasts. Hurricanes, typhoons and other storms could happen more often, causing destruction along the shores. Today's coastal flood defences, such as sea walls and estuary barriers, will be overwhelmed.

▼ Recycled materials can be used as sea walls to protect against rising sea levels – but they only last a few years.

INDEX

Entries in **bold** refer to main subject entries. Entries in *italics* refer to illustrations.

ACKNOWLEDGEMENTS

All artworks are from the Miles Kelly Artwork Bank

The publishers would like to thank the following sources
for the use of their photographs:
t = top, b = bottom, l = left, r = right, c = centre

Alamy Page 49 WaterFrame; 117(t) David Lyons; 118(b) Tibor Bognar

Ardea Pages 24–25 Pat Morris; 83 Kurt Amsler; 86-87 Bill Coster;
90(b) Mark Boulton; 96(t) Jean Paul Ferrero, (b) Valerie Taylor; 97 John Daniels;
98–99(b) David Dixon; 102(br) John Mason; 104 Mark Boulton;
105(b) Dae Sasitorn; 106 Jean Paul Ferrero, (br) M. Watson; 107(b) Valerie
Taylor; 108(t) Mark Boulton, (b) Johan de Meester; 113(t) Jean Paul Ferrero;
120–121 Jean Paul Ferrero; 124-125 Bob Gibbons; 124(t) Thomas Dressier;
125(b) Duncan Usher

Cathy Miles Page 92(bg)

Corbis Page 23 Ralph White; 56(b) Frans Lanting; 78 Stephen
Frink; 116(b) Choo Youn-Kong/Pool/Reuters

Dreamstime.com Page 14(t) Tommy Schultz; 54 (tr) Frhojdysz,
(l) Vintrom; 55(tr) Brento, (br) Ajalbert; 68(c) Goodolga,
(b) Surub; 74(br) Johnandersonphoto; 76(t) Donsimon;
80(t) Stephankerkhofs, (b) Djmattaar

FLPA Page 17(b) Fred Bavendam/Minden Pictures; 34(t) Ingo
Arndt/Minden Pictures, (b) Norbert Wu/Minden Pictures;
41 Norbert Wu/Minden Pictures; 43(b) ImageBroker/
Imagebroker; 62(b) Mike Parry/Minden Pictures;
115(b) D P Wilson; 117(br) ImageBroker/Imagebroker

Fotolia Page 14(c) Tommy Schultz; 15 Desertdiver; 16–17 cornelius;
36(t) zebra0209; 55(bl) Ilan Ben Tov; 57 Vladimir Ovchinnikov;
61(tr) khz; 65(t) Peter Schinck; 69(tl) cbpix; 88(t) Deborah Benbrook;
91(tr) Michael Siller; 102 EcoView; 107(tr) Vladimir Ovchinnikov;
111(br) Vatikaki; 120(tr) Ian Scott, (l) Maribell

Getty Images Page 22(b) Jean Tresfon; 43(t) Neil Bromhall; 79 Jeff Hunter;
103(t) Brian J. Skerry; 122–123 Bloomberg via Getty Images; 123(t) Grant
Duncan-Smith

iStockphoto Pages 14-15 MiguelAngeloSilva; 14(b) tswinner; 36(b) sethakan;
54(br) Dave Bluck; 55(tl) Anders Nygren; 63(bl) TSWinner; 65 Allister Clark;
75(br) Olga Khoroshunova; 91(tl) shayes17; 114(tr) nealec; 119(bl) egdigital;
121(br) igs942

NASA Page 85(t)

Naturepl.com Page 25 Brandon Cole; 37 David Shale; 50 Jeff Rotman;
77 Jurgen Freund; 81 Georgette Douwma

NOAA Page 12(l) W. H. F. Smith; 27(c) Archival Photography by
Steve Nicklas NOS, NGS; 31 NOAA Office of Ocean Exploration,
Dr. Bob Embley, NOAA PMEL; 33 Brooke et al, NOAA-OE,
HBOI; 38(l) Edie Widder

OceanwideImages.com Page 44(c) Gary Bell; 62(tr) Gary Bell

Photolibrary.com Page 39 Reinhard Dirscherl; 48(bl) Paul Kay;
60 Paul Kay; 66 Monica & Michael Sweet; 67 Dana Edmunds;
74–75 Juniors Bildarchiv; 76(b) Wolfgang Poelzer; 84 Franco Banfi;
85(r) Reinhard Dirscherl

Rex Features Page 42(c) W. Disney/Everett

Science Photo Library Pages 8-9 Dr Ken Macdonald;
46–47 Georgette Douwma; 48(tr) Planetobserver; 82 Georgette
Douwma; 123(b) Martin Bond

All other photographs are from: Corel, digitalSTOCK, digitalvision,
ImageState, iStockphoto.com, John Foxx, PhotoAlto, PhotoDisc,
PhotoEssentials, PhotoPro, Stockbyte

Every effort has been made to acknowledge the source and copyright holder of
each picture. Miles Kelly Publishing apologises for any unintentional errors or
omissions.